MYRICK MEMORIES
From Plantation to Town:
1900-1960

ISBN-13: 978-0-9842626-6-3
ISBN-10: 0-9842626-6-0

First printing, October 2010

Cover design by Susan Lindsley and ThomasMax.

Front cover depicts (left to right) Allie, Susan, Lillas

Published by:

 tm

ThomasMax Publishing
P.O. Box 250054
Atlanta, GA 30325
404-794-6588
www.thomasmax.com

MYRICK MEMORIES
From Plantation to Town: 1900-1960
Susan Myrick
Elizabeth "Tippie" Myrick Hubert
Allie Myrick Bowden
Lillas Myrick Lindsley

Susan Lindsley
Editor

ThomasMax

Your Publisher
For The 21st Century

TABLE OF CONTENTS

I. **The Myrick Family**. The parents of the sisters influenced the girls through example, in the home and on the fields of the plantation.

II. **Cousin Gus Myrick**. Sue's story "Who Shall Gather Them?" was probably inspired by the relationship between her cousin Gus and his mistress.

III. **Dr. Hubert** (Tippie's husband) builds an office beside the home.

IV. **The Rockwell Mansion**, home of parents and grandparents, once served as home to a Georgia governor. Its dining room has been moved to the Winterthur Museum in Delaware.

V. **Myrick's Mill** plantation spread over 5,000 acres and was first home of newly wed parents of the authors of these stories.

Photos   93

*For Mary Bowden
and all the children of Dovedale*

ACKNOWLEDGMENTS

Without the assistance of Professor Mary Weatherspoon Bowden, this book would never have been. She provided material, encouragement, and editorial help from the beginning.

Various children of the Myrick family provided photographs and artwork: Susan Warren, Lee Ward, Thulia Bramlett, and Lil James. The watercolor of Myrick's Mill was painted by Katie Myrick Lowerre, sister of the four whose works are included in this book.

Valette Jordan Adkins provided use of the Bethel Church records and helped correct some "misremembered" facts. Betty Dawson donated the picture of the Dovedale post office to the family.

INTRODUCTION

When I was a child, I heard stories about Sherman, a man adored by my mother and her siblings—children of a Confederate veteran. Eventually, I too came to adore Sherman, born to slaves at the close of the War Between the States.

My relatives told me about him and other men and women of their own childhood. Eventually some of the stories became manuscripts for the next generation to learn about life in the early 1900s, in the country, some fourteen miles from the nearest town. The family lived at Dovedale, a one-thousand-acre working plantation northwest of Milledgeville, Georgia, until 1910. About 90 miles southeast of Atlanta, the town was the state capital when General Sherman marched to the sea.

These memories recorded by four of the sisters reveal the joys and hardships of their lives and of the times and also explore the evolving relationships between races up to the 1960s.

The first brief essays are taken from a series of interviews conducted by the editor and by Mary Bowden, Allie Myrick Bowden's daughter-in-law, in the 1970s and 1980s. These describe life on Dovedale Plantation before 1910.

Elizabeth Stith Myrick, the eldest of these four, was born in 1887, and was always called by her nickname, Tippie. She obtained her education at the Dovedale school established by her father, married country doctor Terrell Eugene Hubert in 1905, and became his medical assistant. (See Appendix III.) She earned the added nickname "Turpentine Tippie" because she swabbed turpentine on any injury before the doctor stitched it up. Her writings relate to medicine and child rearing. To her nieces she became more than an aunt and much like a grandmother. Some of Tippie's quotes are probably not original with her, but we have been unable to locate the sources to give credit.

Susan Myrick, born in 1893, also attended the Dovedale school and, after passing a special exam, was admitted to Georgia Normal and Industrial College, called GN&IC, in Milledgeville. She gained fame as the technical adviser of *Gone With The Wind*, for freelance writing, for lectures, and for her newspaper work in several fields, including soil conservation.

The writings of Allie Myrick Bowden inspired this collection.

Born in 1895, she, like her siblings, received her early education at the Dovedale school and then attended GN&IC. After postgraduate studies, she returned to Milledgeville and helped establish the psychology department at GN&IC. In 1923, she married Captain Edwin Bowden (U. S. Army), who was Professor of Military Science and Tactics at the local Georgia Military College.

Lillas Stanley Myrick, the youngest sibling and my mother, followed their leadership in education. After her years at GN&IC, she attended University of Minnesota, the University of Wisconsin and later Columbia University, where she earned her Master's degree and completed her research and course work on nutrition for her doctorate. She took a position in the Chemistry Department at Georgia State College for Women, the new name for GN&IC, where she met Luther C. Lindsley. They married in 1934.

The original language of the writers has been retained to reflect the social conditions at the time of these writings. The editor hopes the reader will not be offended by either the language or events but will accept both as reflecting conditions of the times. Also, the reader should keep in mind that these stories were originally written to be read only by family members.

Editor's Note: Details of family history are provided in Appendix I.

PLANTATION CHILDHOOD
Allie Myrick Bowden

MEAL TIME AT DOVEDALE PLANTATION, ca. 1900

When I was a small child, our morning began with games until we were called to breakfast. We'd play outside games, such as hopscotch, or inside perhaps with paper dolls. We didn't have real paper dolls from the store, like those the children had in the middle of the century. We had to cut ours out of magazines.

We had everything for breakfast—grits always. And eggs any way we wanted them. Every day we had bacon and ham. Sometimes pancakes, and at every meal we had biscuits. Of course, we had Georgia cane syrup made right there at Dovedale.

We had a great cook, Sara Lou. I never saw my mother cook at Dovedale. We children didn't have any kitchen responsibilities until after my father died and we moved to town to the Liberty Street House. Then I wiped the dishes.

Our midday meal, dinner, was the main meal of the day. We always had cornbread and biscuits, chicken, vegetables from the garden in season. The table held everything you could think of for a country meal. But we children just ran into the house and ate and then went back to playing.

When I was about eight, it became my job to set the table, and invariably I'd forget something. So finally, I made me out a list: I can say it right now, knives, forks, spoons, cups, saucers, plates, salt, pepper. I just had to learn all those things; so finally, I wrote them down and put it on the sideboard. And then I stopped having to look at it, I'd just go on.

And was it a big table! There were ten of us, you see. Mama and Papa and eight children—not all at the table at once. My grandmother always spent the summer with us. My mother's mother. My father's mother died before I ever knew her. For a couple of years our cousin Nan Whitehurst (Uncle Cincy's daughter) lived with us. We always had some company, from one to five. Mama was the one in her family that all the brothers and sisters looked to; they always came to Mama.

One time Mama's brother, Zollicoffer, had a sick baby, and so they made plans and came—Aunt Minnie and Zollicoffer and Mary, his wife, and the three children and the baby, and they stayed with us. The doctors said they'd done all they could for this baby. They didn't know if the baby was going to live or not. And of course they didn't have all the canned things they have now. He said that baby would have to have goat's milk. So they decided to come to Dovedale, which they did, and we got a goat, and tied the goat far enough from the house so we couldn't smell it. And they had to milk that goat every three hours to feed the baby, cause it had to be fresh, good goat's milk.

We always kept ice, but that milk had to be fresh, almost as close as if having the baby drink from the mother.

I don't think the table was ever set for less than ten. If there were more than ten, the little ones just got a baked potato and waited for the second table.

My father was very strict. We were told ten minutes before mealtime, and you had to have your face and hands washed and hair brushed and then when they called and said it was ready, "Don't you be late!" Oh, no. He was very strict. We had to come in to have the blessing. I don't think we had to sit all the way through the meal while the grown-ups talked, though.

For supper, we used to have something like waffles, or pancakes and grits. We always had grits for supper. And butter. We had butter for everything, home-churned butter.

After supper, we had to wash our dirty feet. We had played outside in bare feet all day. Sherman would fill the large tub on the back porch *(Editor's Note: What we call today a No. 10 washtub, not a bathtub)* and we would all wash our feet in the same water. After we got our feet washed, Susan would hang up the rag and towel, and Fullie would hang up the tub. If Susan didn't get to it first, Fullie would take the towel and throw it way up the hall. She would have to go get it by the time he hung up the tub. He would empty the water and rinse out the tub and hang it up. Katie and I didn't do anything. And neither did Lillas, of course, as the baby.

We did have a bathroom—only one for all that crowd—but it had running water. You see, Papa had laid running water into only one bathroom. And up until I was ten years old, we children just had moveable bathtubs.

Once we were washed up for the night, we could gather around in the kitchen to listen to Sherman's stories.

THE HOUSE AND THE CROWD

Our house, a one-story, was big enough to crowd the entire family in. The youngest children (Lillas and Katie) slept in a room off Mama and Papa's, and Sue and I doubled up. Everybody else had their own room.

The front door opened into a hall that ran down the length of the house, with rooms on either side. The dining room was separate, at the right-hand end. The children were spread out—somebody seemed to always be away at school. And in that day, everybody left home when they were ready for high school, usually about fourteen.

Since there was no high school were we lived, everyone had to go somewhere and board—often with Uncle Sun, Mother's brother, who lived in Sparta, where they'd go to high school.

The house faced northward, toward the road now called Stiles Cemetery Road. Its roof was shingles (cedar shakes) rather than tin. All of the porches were covered.

We made ice cream in the service area, where we kept the ice chest packed with 200 pounds of ice smothered in sawdust. From the outside door to the service area we could reach the garden.

I remember a cemetery behind the house because I was always scared when I passed by as I went to gather strawberries or wild plums. I think families of people who worked or Papa and Mama were buried there.

We moved to town in 1910, shortly after Papa's death.

The Dovedale house burned in 1931, not long before Mama died. She was heartbroken.

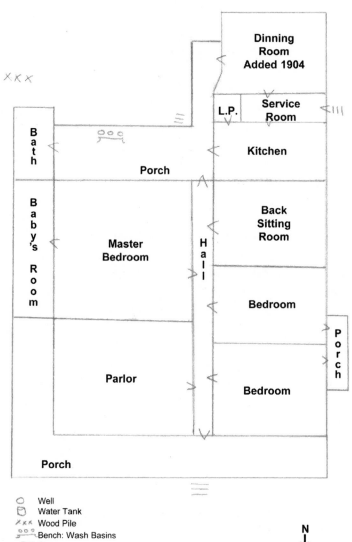

Dinning Room Added 1904

L.P.

Service Room

Kitchen

B a t h

Porch

B a b y 's R o o m

Master Bedroom

H a l l

Back Sitting Room

Bedroom

P o r c h

Parlor

Bedroom

Porch

○ Well
◙ Water Tank
✗✗✗ Wood Pile
~ Bench: Wash Basins
~ Steps
L.P. Locked Pantry

N
↓

not to scale

BUGGIES AND CARS

As a child, Susan always rode behind Papa and hung onto him, but later she rode alone. No one ever taught her how—she just got on the horse and rode. I remember one time Papa had to get a message to Mr. John Tom Williams, who lived about six miles from us. There was nobody else to take the message so Sue got on the horse and took it. And boy, she just thought she was something.

I well remember it, because I was jealous that I couldn't go and take a message. She must have been, I would say, about fourteen maybe. But she had learned to ride a horse, and they were willing to let her go by herself. After that, she and I used to ride some, with me riding behind her.

We didn't have a saddle—Tippie had a side saddle, but we just rode bareback. No jodhpurs or Levis or overalls for girls in that day. When we were children we just rode with whatever we had on—in those days, girls wore dresses all the time, wherever they went, whatever they did. We just got on the horse and rode. I don't know why we didn't blister.

I remember the first time we met an automobile. We were in the carriage, me, Katie and Lil, and Sue was driving. The narrow, unpaved road slashed down long red hills—boy! We were coming down, and going up that hill was a little red Maxwell, the kind of car they had then. Our horses had never seen a car, and they reared up and snorted and all of us got spilled out onto the road, but Sue never turned those reins loose. She held on until the automobile got out of the way and we got back in the carriage.

We were going to the ice cream festival down at Old Bethel. That was the way we made money in those days, because ice cream was a great rarity. They'd have all these big churns around and make the ice cream. They'd make the ice cream and then, I think, every child would pay a nickel for a cup of ice cream, or maybe a penny, I don't know. This was before cones—whoever brought the ice cream also brought some kind of dish to serve it in.

HOUSEHOLD HELP

In that day, people had regular servants. You never had any money, but you had lots of good food, and you had plenty of servants.

Of course Sara Lou, the cook, was one of our favorites.

And Sherman, I don't know exactly what you'd call him. He worked around the house, not on the farm, and he would do things in the house. Although he would do some things outside, like cut up wood for the fireplaces. We all just loved Sherman because he was just so good to us. At night he would come in after sawing wood, or chopping wood, or taking it to the rooms or something. Sherman would come in at suppertime, he'd wash his hands, while we were all washing ours, and he went and got cleaned up. Then he came in and sat in the kitchen—he had a regular chair there, behind a big old iron stove. And so he'd get seated, and we'd all come running; the little ones, would crawl up in his lap, the others just sit on the floor. And he would proceed to tell us about the animals. We just loved those stories.

I learned years later that Joel Chandler Harris wrote these stories down in a collection and credited them to "Uncle Remus." But I credit Sherman, for these were his stories, handed down to him from his family.

GAME TIME

We girls played games all the time. We played everything. And particularly, we played a game called Flinch. I'm sure you've never heard of it. We'd play Flinch by the hour. We didn't play it with regular playing cards. We had Flinch cards. Two, three or four could play. Day and night, well, not so much at night, cause we went to bed more according to the sun. But we played it all the summer. We had a big porch across the front of the house, and we'd go out there on the porch and play Flinch. (*Editor's Note: Flinch cards are still available.*)

We played a lot of other games. Some other card game, not Flinch, but I can't remember the name. Lillas would always win. Always win. She just could do it.

Of course, we played dolls, paper dolls particularly. My mother took a couple of magazines, one the *Ladies' Home Journal*, the other some fashion magazine. We had families, the mother, father, and all the children cut from these magazines. I remember, as I got older, I didn't want to play with paper dolls. And Lil and Katie were still playing. They'd come begging me to join them, and I wouldn't want to. So, one day, I said, okay, so I got me a Papa doll, and then the Papa doll came in, and he stole everything in the house. So then they didn't want to play with me anymore.

We used to make books, called "Possible History." Each one of us had a "Possible History." For example, we'd find a picture of a baby and call it, "Lil was born, at such and such a time." Pictures of students in school, none of them real, just pictures cut out of a magazine. We'd go on in our imagination to their wedding and their children; I don't think they ever had any grandchildren. Things like that—we had to amuse ourselves.

We read a lot. My mother took the **Youth's Companion**, which came out once a week, and everybody wanted to get it, cause it had good, good stories in it. So, whoever could get it first took it to read, and went and hid so she could read before anyone else could get it.

There were no libraries; there were no movies, nothing but family stuff, so we read everything that Dickens ever wrote, because Mama had all those Dickens books. I think David Copperfield was one of our favorite books. When I was the age of Stacey (her granddaughter, then ten) we were reading David Copperfield and Nicholas Nicklebly. Those were my two favorites.

We had a tennis court built when we got older, and we'd play tennis.

AN ATYPICAL BABY SISTER

Lillas could do anything outside, and so you would be surprised that she would make the most delicate, beautiful handkerchiefs. Sometimes they were hemstitched, different things. In that day, we didn't have Kleenex. She had a stack about that [6 inches] high of these that she'd made. And the rest of us, we didn't make handkerchiefs. But whenever we went anywhere, the last thing was to get a handkerchief. And if we didn't have one, we'd get one of Lillas's.

And then one day, I pulled open the drawer, and there's a big placard, that almost covered the drawer. "You know you did wrong to open this drawer." And one by one, everyone went in to get a handkerchief, and would just shut the drawer.

A BROTHER'S FUN

Jim would catch frogs and feed them shotgun pellets (b-b's) and then hold them by the legs and shake out the pellets.

THE LIVESTOCK

When I got up a little in years, it was my job to feed the turkeys and to run down the one we were to have for Thanksgiving. We had cows and horses—I don't know how many horses because we had the carriage, so we had those two horses—for when the family would go to Sunday school. We had the one-horse buggy, just to carry the children, so that's three horses. My father, of course, had his own riding horse. And then we had Lady, gentle enough for the children to ride. I don't know how many oxen and mules to work the fields. Of course, to get the milk, we had milk cows. And dogs, you know, but they never came in the house.

But I tell you, it's a different life now. You were asking about ice. When we lived in the country, we bought two hundred pounds once a week. We had to go into Milledgeville to buy it, in the wagon drawn by mules. They wrapped it up in burlap, put it in an old wooden chest, packed that in sawdust, and brought it home in the wagon. We didn't have an ice house, so it was kept on the back porch. We just chopped it off as we wanted it.

We had a big cellar we used for many things. Papa loved to experiment with trees. And we had I don't know how many varieties of figs. Oh, they were the best figs! We had pear trees and apples and peaches by the millions.

POST OFFICE AND SCHOOLS

My family ran the post office at Dovedale, and my father built the schools.

He built a church for the Negroes, where my land joins the Stiles line (on Stiles cemetery Road, west of the junction with Stiles Road) and gave them a deed to the church and so much land, I don't know how much. The deed was recorded, and it was theirs as long as it was used for a church. And when it was not, it was to revert to the family. Of course the church went out of existence, I don't even remember it as a church, but when it stopped being a church, it was used as a schoolhouse. When the school closed, the land went back to the Myrick family.

Editor's Note: He built a school for the white children and one for the black children of the area, both on Dovedale land.

The post office, Dovedale, Georgia, operated from 29 July 1886 to 15 February 19ll. Mrs. Thulia K. Myrick was appointed postmaster on 29 July 1886.

##

THANKSGIVING

We always got together for Thanksgiving, always had a big dinner. But a couple of years after we moved to Milledgeville, I guess I was sixteen, seventeen, my mother said, "This is the last time I'm going to have Thanksgiving dinner. Everybody is in such a hurry to get over to Georgia Military College (GMC) to see the ball game. I'm not going to spend the whole morning getting dinner and then you just gobble it up and run."

That football game was something we looked forward to. I don't know how long that lasted, but they had ball games over there from the time we moved to Milledgeville, 1910. Everybody went.

THE BOUDOIR CAP REMEMBERED

The boudoir cap round robin started in Milledgeville. With Lillas. I think it was the last Christmas that I was at home, before I was married. So that was in 1922. Lillas was the baby of the family. That Christmas Eve night, the tree was all fixed, the presents were all around it.

And Lillas said, "I want to open one package."

"No, no, we'll get them all tomorrow," Mama said.

Well, of course Lillas was always smaller, and so finally Mama said, "All right, we'll let Lillas open one package, but no one else can open any packages."

She chose a package, about 18" x 18" and about one inch thick, opened it, and it was a boudoir cap. And Lillas was not the type for a boudoir cap. None of us could ever imagine her with a boudoir cap! Well, we had hysterics.

Lillas said, "I'm going down to the post office."

Things were different then, post offices stayed open. She wrapped it all back up, and mailed it to Nan [Nan Whitehurst, her cousin].

Special Delivery.   That started it.   And then Nan sent it the next Christmas to one of us. And it kept going. Lillas had it when Westover [her home] burned in 1954, and so ended its journeys around the world, from Canada to Hawaii and all over the states.

Editor's Note: Several versions of the origination of this "gift" have passed around the family. Lillas (mother of the editor) began the game. She often said that she initially received it from her cousin Nan Whitehurst (Ingram), opened it on Christmas Eve, re-wrapped it that night, changed the gift tag to red "From Lil, to Nan," added the words "I hope this reaches you in time to pass on," and presented it back to Nan on Christmas morning.

ASTRIDE THE MASON-DIXON LINE
Allie Myrick Bowden
1923

A few weeks ago, a Northern lady, who seemed fascinated by my accent and curious about many Southern customs, asked me, "Why do all Southern people hate Negroes so?"

She left me pondering her belief that I could hate the Negroes. How could she have such an idea?

Could I hate Aunt Minerva, a veritable Mammy who had cared for all of us when we were small children? Aunt Minerva who, when my father died and we moved to town and the children were all in school, went to work for another family, but came to see us often and called us her "chillun" (the others she merely took care of). Hate Aunt Minerva? Why, only a few short weeks ago I had been proud to have her as a guest in the balcony of the church when I was married.

And Sherman? Sherman was first named John Henry Calhoun, a name which he used for the address on a paper that came to him regularly once a week as long as he lived, though he could read no word of it. John Henry Calhoun was just a baby when Sherman marched through Georgia, and so his name was changed to commemorate the event. Sherman it was forever, except on that strange paper.

In New York, Sherman would be called the "yard man," but to us he was just Sherman who worked the garden, the flower beds, cut the grass, did odd jobs around the house, and always had peanuts or scaly barks in his pockets. In cold weather he ate his dinner in a corner of the kitchen behind the big wood-burning stove, and no king ever enjoyed a royal feast as he did the collards or turnip greens or cow peas that the cook served to him along with pot liker, corn bread, sweet potatoes, hot biscuits and Georgia cane syrup. He was a small man with the whitest teeth and an almost constant cheerful grin. Somehow he always found time for a story for us and we always found him for the story, behind the stove in winter.

And Mary? Mary cooked for us for years and years. In summer, she would cook outside beneath the pecan trees. When there was company and dinner was late, she would slip us a baked potato, soft and juicy and sweet as sugar. Of course, I mean a sweet potato; the others we designated as Irish potatoes. I am sure whoever first said, "Just take a tater and wait," had a similar experience.

Of course, Mary lived "on the place," which meant she lived in one of the many houses on my father's plantation. It was some forty or more years after the War Between the States when I was a child, and, while there were no longer slave quarters, one never dreamed of having a servant live in their house. Nor did they have one work for them who lived off the place. Consequently, all cooks, nurses, washwomen, or servants of any type had a house with several acres for chickens and a garden somewhere on the plantation. They were usually the wives or dependents of some of the Negro men who, with mules, feed and sideback furnished by my father, planted and raised cotton, corn, sweet potatoes, sugar cane, and peas, and paid him in the fall in bales of cotton for their year's run and rent—two bales of cotton for a one-horse (or mule) farm; four for a two, and so on.

Mary lived about a half mile down the road and after dinner, which was at one o'clock, went home each day, to return about five o'clock to cook supper. Even now it brings delicious thrills to my mind to think of her returning to cook supper on a hot summer's afternoon, walking through the front gate and across the lawn with a big bucket of wild plums balanced on her head. Oh, the cool juiciness of those plums; some red, some yellow, but all tender and sweet and tangy. There were squeals of delight as we children dived in and no one said, "Wait, it will spoil your supper." We ate and ate, and as far as I know they never spoiled our appetite; in fact, I believe they put an extra edge on it, although we never stopped until the bucket was empty—empty, that is, except for several good handfuls for Mattie to eat on her way to take the bucket to the kitchen.

Mattie was the little Negro girl whose job it was to play with us—with me and my sister and numerous little cousins, some of whom were always there on a visit. She spent countless hours swinging us in the big hammocks made of ropes and barrel staves which hung between the large post oaks that furnished pleasant shade as well as support for the swings.

Mattie was a marvel at cutting out paper dolls, fashioning corn shuck dolls, singing to us and making up games for us to play.

She was an expert on peep shows. She would scoop a shallow hole in the sand up close to the great gnarled oak roots that protruded from the ground. Then she arranged flowers, without stems, in this shallow bowl—roses, violets, bleeding heart, red clover, sweet, sticky blooms from the varnish tree, which she had picked. She made a beautiful bouquet in the sand, then she laid a piece of glass over the top and covered it well with sand. The moment had come; we all hopped from one foot to the other.

"Mattie, who's going to peep first?" we asked.

"Got to count out," she unfailingly answered.

We all ran to sit in a circle on the nearby lawn and each little girl quickly spread out ten little chubby fingers. We watched Mattie as she counted, touching a finger with each word. She chanted:

> "William, William Trimble toe
> He's a good fisherman,
> Catches his hens,
> Puts 'em in pens
> Some lay eggs
> And some do not
> Wire, brier, limberlock
> Sit and sing till ten o'clock
> Clock runs round
> Mouse runs down
> O U T spells
> Out to Uncle Jack's house
> You dirty dish rag
> YOU!"

We all jumped up and rushed headlong to watch enviously while Mattie drew a line in the sand that nobody dared cross except the one who had been counted out. The chosen one ran to the spot and squatted there to watch breathlessly as Mattie pushed the sand back carefully to make a clear, clean circle. Into the circle peeped the first of us, "Oh-ing" and "Ah-ing," over the bouquet's beauty. The rest of us returned to the counting circle until each of us had viewed the peep show. I never visit a flower show with its many flower arrangements that my thoughts do not return to Mattie and her colorful bowls in the sand.

And Jenny! Jenny, I know, was my mother's greatest joy, next to Mary, who could always have the biscuits and muffins hot. For it was Jenny who each week washed so white, starched so stiff, and ironed so smooth the endless number of petticoats, pantalets and dresses that little girls wore in those days. From Monday morning till Thursday night she worked on the clothes. On Friday morning she drove the quarter mile to the house in a one-horse wagon, the basket piled high not only with the little girls' clothes, but also dozens of snowy white napkins, tablecloths, sheets, towels and my father's stiffly starched shirts.

Hate Jenny? Never. A few of her children (there were fourteen of them, with only six bearing the same surname), however, were a trial. One, Hezekiah Freeman, acted as a kind of butler and water boy. Although we had a hydraulic pump which furnished water from the spring for bathing and cooking, there was a constant demand for fresh, cool well water for drinking. In addition to his other varied duties, Hezekiah was supposed to be available at any moment to draw a fresh bucket of water. But he was not only lazy and trifling, but also often managed to be out of the way when fresh water was wanted. Another of Mary's sons, Will Collier, only half-curried the horses, thus provoking my father's wrath. Another, Robert Liptrot, stole corn from the barn and sold it to a neighboring store to spend the money on a few "draps." And another, Lougene (named for my cousin Eugene) stole the finest watermelons from the patch every year. But we managed to deal with these problems and they furnished fun as well as provocation to my parents.

When I was older, there was one whom I almost hated for a moment—at least, I was terribly angry with her. It was two days before Christmas. We were all young ladies and no longer lived on the plantation but in town. Our cook was a town Negro named Liza. The man whom I expected some day to marry was coming the next day. Many preparations had already been made: A twenty-pound turkey was dressed and ready in the ice box; a huge fruit cake had been baked weeks earlier. That day, Liza and my mother had baked a nut cake, rich with Georgia pecans, a chocolate cake and a lemon cheesecake—all made with plenty of butter and eggs so that they would be soft and fresh and light as long as they lasted. There was no Swansdowns cake flour (Ed: self-rising), and baking powder cakes had to be eaten the very first day. There was also a pound cake, a traditional gift of an aunt and uncle in the country, who also sent long links of freshly ground sausage. Plum pudding was no Christmas dish with us; instead, we must have varied cakes to accompany that dish of all dishes for Christmas day—Ambrosia—made from almost freshly picked oranges from Florida and piles of grated, not ground, fresh cocoanut.

The cakes were made, but there was greater excitement than usual that Christmas, and much remained to be done. As Liza started out that night, she asked to speak to my mother and then said in a low, quiet voice, "Miss Kate, I won't be here tomorrow. I'se gittin' married." Not an inkling of this heretofore.

It was a major calamity. For a moment I did hate Liza with a sharp fierce hatred that she should so unfairly walk out on my mother that way. Christmas and no cook! It meant my mother must stand long hours over a hot stove to prepare the traditional Christmas dinner. There were four of us girls, and we could help by setting the table, making the salad, slicing the cake, arranging relishes and such easy tasks that had more to do with beauty and attractiveness of the table than actual preparation of food, but further than that we could not go. For, like all the other Southern girls, we were not taught to work. It was not necessary; we only knew how to have some one else do it correctly. Yet, strangely enough, we unconsciously were taught that when married life demanded it of us, we must take hold and do a good job of homemaking with or without help.

The girl that Liza sent to take her place that day turned out to be a fairly good cook, so I did not hate Liza so much after all. When, during dinner, the girl came into the dining room in her stocking feet because her shoes hurt, she occasioned so much merriment that any faults were completely forgotten as was all anger toward Liza.

I keep recalling so many Negroes that we knew so well as servants or renters for so long. Often, when I see a beautiful sunset or we have a refreshing rain after days of dry, scorching weather, I think of old Uncle Martin, now dead. For many years after we grew up, he came several times each week to help my mother in her flower garden. He did it so well and loved the flowers so much that they seemed to grow more beautifully for him. I am sure he is tending flowers somewhere in heaven today.

TINKER BELL
Lillas S. Myrick Lindsley
1929

Wanted: A passenger. Driving to Georgia or Florida in Pontiac roadster. Desire someone for company and to share expenses. Leaving middle of June. P. O. Box 4485.

"Interested in driving with you if you go anywhere near Baltimore. Jack. P.O. Box 6872."

"Would like to go to Alabama with you. Have made trip before and could help with driving. I'm a female. Hope you are same species. Julie. P.O. Box 2684. Phone: Dismore 2795."

"Am a widower, 25 years old. Going to Miami and would like to go with you are far as you go. Phone MI-6687."

"I'm a P.E. major, junior. If you'll take me to Memphis, I'll go with you. Come to see me at 1268 Fourth Avenue."

Such were the answers received from my want ad posted on the bulletin board in the post office of the University of Minnesota. Only a week before I would leave for home, and all these applicants to be interviewed! Alas! None of them proved successful. Consequently, I jumped at the idea when one of my professors said he was going to Chicago and would be glad to accompany me that far.

Exams, last minute parties, and, in the midst of good-byes, I began packing Tinker Bell. That was the name I gave the Pontiac, since it flies around everywhere. It seemed to possess everything except a kitchen stove and a piano. With much assistance and struggling, however, I managed to tie everything that wouldn't go into the trunk and rumble seat on top of them. I then parked Tinker Bell by the side of Sanford dorm, ready to leave early in the morning.

The old alarm clock sounded fifteen minutes after my head hit the pillow. In less time than that, I crept down the stairs while it was not quite light. The prof joined me, and then homeward bound. We were away from the city just as it was waking. I talked intellectually for miles and miles. On across Wisconsin, and the close of the first day found us in Chicago after 500 miles more or less.

I was cordially received by friends and forgot hot dusty roads and detours. Yet, with the dawn of another day, maps and more maps were unfolded, routes and more routes traced, suggestions and more suggestions received. Finally it was decided that I should take Nation No. 41. So manfully and fearlessly, I started out, accompanied by two French dolls. Toodles was stylishly dressed in high heels and long skirt, while Flatateena wore pajamas. By sitting on top of the portable Victrola on the seat, they had a ringside view.

Chicago traffic on Sunday morning seemed, at first, impenetrable, but Tinker Bell stayed on Route 41 and was soon speeding on toward Indianapolis, then away from Indianapolis. Sunset found us at Frankly, Indiana, a tourist town. We made 260 miles.

A bell ringing jarred me awake and someone said, "You asked to be called at five o'clock."

Half awake and half asleep, I headed for Louisville.
M-I-N-N-E-S-O-T-A
Minnesota! Minnesota!
Yes, Gopher!

No longer was I sleepy or lonesome, for I had the University of Minnesota band with me.
Minnesota, hail to thee!
Hail to thee, our College dear!
Thy light shall ever be
A beacon bright and clear;
Thy sons and daughters true
Will proclaim thee near and far
They will guard thy name;
And adore thy name;
Thou shall be their Northern star.

The Alma Mater, and I couldn't stand! No chance of getting lonesome, for when the band left, I had Rudy Vallee and the Boob Boop A Doop girl along. For I found that I could crank the portable Vic on the seat beside me and have music as I rode along.

At last, in the blue grass region of Kentucky. It was again time to feed Tinker Bell. I never gave her more than five galloons of gas at a time, so I could have an excuse to stop often and talk to someone. Having had little chance to see a newspaper, I was dumbfounded to see the extreme drought. At a Louisville filling station, I inquired, "It is this dry all over Kentucky?"

He replied, "Why, lady, it ain't dry. I kin git you ten gallons in ten minutes."

Later I was advised that going through Stanton and Ashville, instead of Nashville and Chattanooga, would shorten my route considerable. Willingly, I accepted the advice and started out in that direction. After going about thirty miles, I thought I should be somewhere near a town so I stopped the first person I met and asked, "How far to Shelbyville?"

"You're going the wrong way. It's on the other side of Louisville."

Realizing I took the right highway but had gone the wrong direction, I asked, "Well, where does this road go?"

"To Elizabeth."

"And on to Nashville?"

"Yes."

"Thanks," I said. "I'll just go to Nashville."

The man looked at me and shook his head, as though I needed more assistance than he could give me. But after all, what difference did it make which way I went?

I drove on.

After leaving Nashville, I soon reached the Appalachian Mountains. Just a gradual incline, around curves, and more curves, and then down, and soon I was across one mountain and ready to start the next. With the car top back and the windshield down in the late afternoon, it was "boop, boop, a doop." If the curve was just right, the Vic played double quick time; if the curve turned the other direction, it played backwards.

When I reached the Georgia line, I felt as thought I were really home. The first person I talked to noticed my Minnesota license plate and said, "You sho' are a far way from home. Going to Florida?"

Finally at home, I pitched bags and baggage into the house, and at 4:30 a.m. I started out for Daytona Beach to join my family. On through Jacksonville and to St. Augustine, where I took the ocean boulevard. At last, after miles and days, I arrived at the end of a 440-

mile day.

I drove from one end of Atlantic Avenue to the other and half way back before I found number 353. Just as I stopped, my five-year-old red-headed nephew ran out and shouted, "Here's Lil," at the top of his voice.

The first question was "Who came with you?"

Then I couldn't tell it fast enough—company for the 550 miles to Chicago in one day; but the rest of the trip alone (apologies to Toodles and Flatateena). The next day, 260 miles, starting out after 10 a.m., then 340 miles the next, 250 to Atlanta, and another 100 to Milledgeville, and then 440 to Daytona. Only 1500 miles!

The most famous beach in America, a playground for all. The baby in his sunsuit (as the prof who rode with me to Chicago would say, "activates his ergosterol"), granddad in his bathing suit and sis in her beach pajamas. Here for a month I frolicked, rode the waves, bathed in the sun and rode up the beach to the lighthouse where the crabs were thickest, across to the inlet where the big fish bite, and back to the cottage to eat and sleep.

I started for home early one morning. This time my mother was with me. When we reached the Florida line, we were stopped by uniformed men "to be inspected."

"For bugs?" I asked.

"Do you have any fruit or plants?"

"Yes," I said hesitatingly. Feeling like a bootlegger, I confessed and handed over my tree orchids I had found in the woods after a day's hunt. I also handed over a bag of oranges.

"Would you mind getting out, lady?" he asked as he pitched my orchids, which I treasured so, and my fruit onto the ground. Then he searched under the seat and actually opened the suitcases as though I had more hidden away.

"All right," he called out as he put on the inspection seal.

"Hope you enjoy the orange juice," I called out as I drove off, and then wondered why I hadn't just stayed and eaten some.

I began a rapid conversation with Mother, lest she should realize I was somewhat disgruntled with having to part with the orchids. Then the landscape began to show Georgia around us, and when I saw a roadside stand with baskets running over with peaches, I felt the thrill of home, my native land as the words came to me.

When you see the cotton blooming and the fields of waving grain,
Then you know you're in Georgia land.
When the wind sighs through the pine trees as you stroll down
          lovers' lane,
When you hear the banjos tuning and all the children dance
In the moonlight near the cabin doors
And you feel so free and happy, then you know you've reached the
          land,
Georgia land,
Where milk and honey flows.

Oh, Georgia with your hedges of Cherokee abloom
Your watermelons, peaches and goldenrod's tall plume.
You're dearest and nearest, in my heart your beauty glows.
Oh, Georgia land, my Georgia land, where milk and honey flows.

———————

Editor's note: We could not locate the source of this quotation.

TIPPPIE'S POT POURI
Elizabeth Myrick Hubert
Dates unknown

MEDICAL ADVICE

As a physician's wife, Tippie heard many comments about medicine. Some are well-known, others not. The most famous is "an apple a day keeps the doctor away."

While there is life, there is hope.

Not all diseases are bad—some provide the cure.

Prevention is next to Godliness.

If you can't be good, be careful.

Light meals ensure a long life.

The cure is often worse than the disease.

When colds are rife, avoid a crowd.

It's easy to catch a disease in a crowd.

If you would heal your eye, your hands you must tie.

It is better to have a lucky doctor than a learned one.

The doctor is more to be feared than the disease.

After dinner (lunch) rest a while, after supper, walk a mile.

The sick person who doesn't get well is getting worse.

Heaven help us from an apothecary's mistake.

Trying to cure yourself will ruin you.

There is no medicine to cure stupidity.

What is new is not necessarily true.

He is a fool who makes his doctor his heir.

POPCORN NIGHTS

Often on a cold day, late in the afternoon, we children would shout for joy to see our father come from the barn with a basket of corn cobs on his arm and his pockets bulging with popcorn. He piled the cobs on the fire to make coals over which to pop the corn.

We children sat on the floor and shelled the corn into our aprons. Our father popped the corn and often he would say:

Take two ears of yellow corn, or red
Then rub, rub, rub till the kernels
All rattle from the nub, nub, nub.
Then put them in popper made of wire, wire, wire,
And hold the little popper over the fire, fire, fire.
When the corn begins to pop give it a shake, shake, shake
And then a pretty clatter it will make, make, make,
When it all turns white you will know the popping
Is done right, right, right.
Then pour it in a platter
For it is done, done, done.
Pass the platter round
And that's the fun, fun, fun.

ICE CREAM TIMES

We lived twelve mile from Milledgeville and the only way to get ice in summer was to buy a 200-pound block from the ice house twelve miles away, wrap it in a blanket and haul it in a wagon. When it arrived at home, it was put in the cellar and covered with wood shavings and blankets.

Our mother would have the rich yellow custard ready made, and cooled, and the ice cream churn and salt waiting. She put the churn into the freezer, and then came our fun of cracking off the ice in small pieces with a big nail and a hammer. First about two inches of ice were put into the freezer and then covered with a layer of salt; we alternated these layers until salt and ice filled the freezer.

My brother and I took turns cranking the freezer. In about 20 minutes the cream was frozen. Mother would take out the blades, repack everything, and cover it all with a blanket until time for the ice cream to be served. Mother, Father, Grandmother, and eight children soon ate and ate, until they ate it all up.

If you have never eaten homemade ice cream, you don't know what good ice cream is. We often flavored ours with figs or peaches grown on the farm.

———————————————

Editor's note: Tippie's home-churned ice cream always included raw eggs. Today, the risk of getting salmonella from raw eggs is considered high, but in those days, we just washed the eggs after we gathered them from the hen house, and using them raw in the ice cream didn't present any problem.

Tippie's Home-Churned Ice Cream: *Beat 4 eggs; gradually add 2 cups sugar while beating until mixture gets thick. Add 1 12-ounce can Carnation milk, 1 14-ounce can Eagle Brand milk, a pinch of salt and 2 teaspoons vanilla, mixing thoroughly. Pour into freezer churn and add enough whole milk to bring to the "fill" line. Churn, adding salt to the ice, until the mixture hardens. Keep packed in ice until served.*

RIDDLES AND GIGGLES FOR THE YOUNG

A Goose, a Fox and a Peck of Corn

While carrying a goose, a fox and a peck of corn in an open box, a man had to cross a creek on a foot log. He could tote only one across at a time. If he took the corn first, the fox would eat the goose. If he took the fox first, the goose would eat the corn.
How did he take them across?
> The goose first, then the corn. Take the goose back and get the fox. Then go back for the goose

Six set, seven sprung, from the dead the living run.
> A hen set on six eggs.

What do bees do with their honey?
> Cell it

Why do you always put your left shoe on last?
> When you put one on, the other is always left.

Why is an angry man like 12:59 o'clock?
> Because he is ready to strike one.

What did the doughnut say to the loaf of bread?
> If I had your dough I wouldn't be hanging around this hole.

What made the wood duck duck?
> She was afraid the woodpecker would peck her.

What is horse sense?
> Stable thinking

What fish cannot be charged?
> C O D

How many fish did the commercial fisherman toss back, and why?
> One smelt, it wasn't worth a (s)cent.

What is the first thing a shoemaker needs to make a shoe?
> The last

Why do cows have bells?
> Their horns don't work.

What would you call a tailor if you don't know his name?
> Mr. Sew and Sew

What goes up when the rain comes down?
> An umbrella

What can go up the chimney down but can't go down the chimney up?
> An umbrella

What did the stuck elevator say?
> I'm coming down with something.

What must one do to have soft hands?
> Nothing

What's peculiar about a man darning his socks?
> His hands are where his feet should be

What kind of robber isn't dangerous?
> A safe robber

What is worse than "raining cats and dogs"?
> Hailing taxies

What word do women like best?
> The last word

How much are your ten dollar shoes worth?
> Five dollars a foot.

Why is 1,000,000 a bad number?
> It's so "naughty"

What baseball players are always in the kitchen?
> The batter and the pitcher.

Why is tennis such a noisy game?
>Because each player raises a racket

Why should a golf player wear two pairs of pants?
>Because he might make a hole in one

What girl's name is a Christmas song?
>Carol

Why are bells so obedient?
>Because they ring when they are tolled

What flies and whistles and won't eat bird seed?
>A plane

What color is a child when you spank him?
>Yell-o

Start with nothing, add your age, double the result, add ten, divide by two, subtract your age, and subtract 5. What do you have?
>Nothing

What food is dear at any price?
>Venison

Who does the cork call when it is removed from the bottle?
>Pop

When is a doctor annoyed?
>When he is out of patients

Why should a dishonest man always stay indoors?
>So he won't be found out

What did the picture say to the wall?
>First they framed me and then they hung me

What would you do if you found Chicago Ill?
>Call Baltimore MD

What lives in the winter, dies in summer and grows with its roots upward?

> An icicle

Which kind of building holds the most corn?

> A corn-dominium

TONGUE TWISTERS

These should be repeated at least three times, aloud and rapidly:

Slim sawed six slick, slim saplings.

Every single shingle shrunk.

The skunk sat on the stump. The skunk thought that the stump stunk and the stump thought that the skunk stunk.

She sells sea shells by the sea shore.

MORE THOUGHTFUL RIDDLES

Two men were sitting together when a young man passed by. Said one to the other, "Who is that young man?" The other replied, "Brothers and sisters have I none, but that man's father is my father's son."

> *The speaker's son.*

Two geese in front of two geese, two geese behind two geese, two geese between two geese. How many geese?

> *Four (Not six)*

Punctuate:

That that is is that that is not is not is not that it it is.

I want more space between pig and and and and and whistle.

A LITTLE ARITHMATIC

Write any number between 100 and 1000, but each numeral must be
one less than the digit to its left.   e. g.,   543
Reverse the order of the numerals: 345
Subtract and you'll always get   198

What number doubled is equal to itself added to one?
    One.
Fun to know:
    Add two odd numbers, always get an even number
    Add two even numbers, always get an even number
    Add an even number to an odd number, always get an odd number.

A BIT OF PUZZLE FUN

Fill in the blanks:

A baker who lived in _ _ _ice sold his _ice_ _ cake by the _ _ ice. He
gave _ _ _ ice, in his _ _ _ice that the _ _ice is love for this _ _ _ _ice.

Letter Game (before there was Scrabble):

Use ¼ of the letters in NOSE, 2/3 of the letters in TOE, 1/3 of those in
ARM, ¼ of those in HAIR, ½ of CHIN, to spell another part of the
human body.

GOING COURTING AT 54
Lillas S. Myrick Lindsley
1954

At the age of 54 I was one of the two women called for traverse jury in a small county in Middle Georgia. As soon as women in Georgia were given the privilege of serving I asked that my name be put in the jury box. This was the 5th term of court since my name had been added. There were 55 men, two women, and no Negroes.

It was one of those typical October mornings in Georgia when the air is crispy and crunchy as cereal and by noon is warm and lazy. The coolness made the court room appear cleaner, and I thought it unnecessary when one of the witnesses dusted the bench before sitting down. The sun rays, bright through the unwashed, screenless windows, made the dust seem less thick. The Venetian blinds were only on the west side to stop the afternoon sun; hung at different lengths they appeared lopsided. No one smoked, so the room did not smell of tobacco.

A loudspeaker had been installed for the judge and for the witnesses when testifying. I had no view of the balcony where the Negroes were seated.

On my first day, I came a little early. The jury sauntered in one by one in a gentlemanly, orderly manner, with friendly nods to each other. I knew most of the men, and had known many of them for more than 40 years. They were farmers, merchants, plumbers, insurance men, and salesmen, but no bankers or professional men. Only a few were under forty and at least half were my age or older. I imagine it was an old experience for all except "us women." They had an air of boredom and unconcern, the attitude of "it's just a job to be done," rather than one of duty and honor.

Before court was over, however, interest was so high that quite a few members who were not in the box and were excused chose to remain and listen.

The lawyers chatted among themselves, some lined up against the wall near the judges bench and some seated around tables, some coming for a few minutes and leaving, then returning. The older ones showed no interest in the whole affair, but the less experienced were like bright-eyed youngsters waiting for class to start. Every one seemed friendly toward the pretty vivacious lady lawyer.

At ten sharp, the judge in his white-collared dignity entered and asked the sheriff to call the court in session.

"Hi-yaaa, hi-yaaaa..... superior court is now in session."

The clerk of court then called the roll of jurors and we were asked to stand, raise our right hands, and take the Oath, "I do ....so help me God."

Since there were women on the jury, it was necessary to have a woman bailiff, thus a charming young matron was sworn in to serve. As she went to take her seat near the jury box, one of the lawyers in a stage whisper said, "You can take charge of me now." A smile went over the room.

The judge then called the calendar for the term. He gave the case number and the name of plaintiff and defendant, and a lawyer responded as to their readiness: "Plaintiff is ready, Your Honor," or "Settled and dismissed, Your Honor," or "Ready, Your Honor." It was difficult to hear; even the judge opted not to speak directly into the microphone.

While this was going on, since so little could be heard, the jurors whispered among themselves. This whispering continued throughout the court session when the judge and lawyers talked, both before a suit began and while waiting for a witness, or waiting for anything.

What we were waiting for I didn't know most of the time. These conversations about the people involved in suits made it all very entertaining and interesting. Also hearing remarks made by friends not directly to me proved very enlightening.

A man in back of me conversed with a friend from out of town. The friend was wondering why all the delay. The juror told him, "The judge is very cautious. This is the biggest circuit in Georgia. Not another judge who serves in eight or nine counties. Often some cases go till next term of court. Atlanta has six senior judges. They continue until they finish."

I served on the first case that came up. The clerk of court called out twelve names for the jury, and I took a seat on the jury bench. No one was struck because the defendant had not answered the suit filed by a black man for damages to his car in an accident.

A Negro was asking for damages in the amount of $724.00 for

damage to his car in an accident. Race was never mentioned, but our community is small, and almost everyone on the panel recognized the name of the defendant's family—a white family.

The plaintiff gave the evidence, the judge charged us to decide the amount of damages to be paid, and the jury retired. In less than 15 minutes, we reached a decision. The defendant was asked to pay $600.00.

After we left the box and returned to the court room, I heard the remark that it didn't make any difference what amount was set, the Negro would never be able to collect a cent of it—but race had nothing to do with that part.

On the third day, before court opened, a group of us were standing around talking and one of the men stated that he hated to serve on a jury with women, but "I guess it is better than having to serve with niggers."

Numerous visitors came every day to listen to a case of personal interest. Only one man attended every day, sometime alone, sometimes with his wife, sometimes with his son, and sometimes with both. He listened to every word spoken, laughed, nodded an agreement, or gave a look that said, "I knew it." The day a divorce case came up where a difference in religion was the main trouble, many members of the small church were there. In another divorce case where the man had been married before, his ex-wife and her husband were there. It made me think of a cheering section at a ball game. The judge umpired, the jury retired and then came back to announce the winner.

One of the most important things in each case was the striking of the jurors by the two lawyers. At least 30 or 45 minutes was spent in doing so. From the length of time and the seriousness, much seemed to depend on it. With the correct jury picked, the game was half won. There were many things to be considered: Were these prospective jurors friends or enemies to him or to his client? Would they go along with the crowd or have strong convictions? Would they stand up for what they thought was right or be influenced by others? Were they members of the Masonic organization or the Klu (*sic*) Klux Klan? To strike or not to strike. That was the lawyers' decision.

One of the most interesting cases was a damage suit against the city. A woman who had fallen because of a bad place on the sidewalk and had been hospitalized for some time was suing the city to take care of a big doctor's bill and hospital bill. The evidence was brought out by the city engineer that the sidewalk was in need of repair, that it was his duty to inspect the sidewalks from time to time and keep them in shape, that this place needed repair and had not been fixed. The plaintiff was not even granted a penny. The rumor through the courtroom was that she deserved some payment from the city but they (the jurors) could not set a precedent. If so, every time anybody fell and got hurt, they would expect the city to pay. Yet she needed the money and the evidence showed she deserved it.

There was a divorce case where the husband and wife were both in their early 20's. They had a nine-month old child and someone had brought the baby to the court room. It cried out just often enough to keep the court reminded that the baby must be considered. Both parents wanted the child. The girl's church rules did not permit ball playing and the entire divorce revolved around the fact that the husband played at night and left her home alone. My thought went to the fact that these 12 people could decide the fate of that helpless baby's life—whether she lived with her mother or father or divided the time between the two. A divorce was not granted.

On the criminal docket all cases were against Negroes; one for driving under the influence of alcohol, one for attempted robbery, and one for running a gambling house. Each Negro had a white lawyer and I am sure they received as much justice as anyone. One was found not guilty, one was fined $200.00, and the other case was not finished when I left.

The judge was most considerate of the jury members who were not in the box. As each case began he asked the lawyers approximately how long the case would last, and then excused the idle jurors until court resumed at 2 p.m. or till the next morning.

On every other case members were struck from the list and each time my name was called I was struck. None of my family are Masons, none are Klu (*sic*) Klux; all the lawyers were on friendly terms; I knew none of the clients.

I think, however, that I have a reputation for not being easily influenced by others and for standing up for what I think is right. Perhaps that is why I was among the "jurors excused" every time.

So, at the end of four days, having spent 15 minutes in the jury box and room, and any number of hours hanging around the courthouse, I went by the Clerk's Office with the others and drew my pay of $20.00, a much wiser and better informed citizen.

DOVEDALE
Susan Myrick
Event date: Circa 1905

It's a long way in space, time and conditions from Washington, D. C. to Dovedale, Georgia, where I grew up, but reading about an inaugural ball gown brought me recollections of a day in Dovedale.

Miss Carol Channing, the actress, posed for her picture in the gown she will wear to the Inaugural Gala: The feathered hemline is of "rare vulture feathers," the cutlines said.

Now, in Dovedale (population about 73, I reckon) nobody ever called a turkey buzzard a vulture, but they do belong to the same family, so reading of the vulture feathers on Miss Channing's gown, I let my mind drift back to the April Fool's Day when the 18-or-so children of the Dovedale school "ran away from school." Both parents and teachers thought it was quite all right for the children to leave school on that All Fool's Day, but we were scared half to death, just the same, since we didn't know our behavior met with approval of the grownups.

We all took lunch boxes to school, so it was not difficult to sneak them from the shelf where they usually stayed and take them with us when we took off for the woods.

We played games and wandered through the woods, locating last-year's birds' nests, noting the squirrels and rabbits that ran past, in general enjoying the stolen outing in the fashion of all children.

Then, one of our number called out in tones of great excitement for us to come see what he had found. We scrambled over brush and brier and were soon repelled by a horrible stench.

He had found a buzzard's nest.

Despite the smell, we managed not to throw up and got close up to the nest. The mother bird was away, foraging for food, no doubt, but the young birds, all four of them, were in the nest.

That was the shock of my lifetime. The baby buzzards were white.

Until then I had thought a buzzard had to be black. As he flies in the air, far above your head, he seems black against the light, and his soaring circles which let the sun glint from his feathers leave the impression of blackness. I never dreamed the babies were white, and I could hardly believe my father, that evening, when he told me the babies turned black, too.

Did you ever hear the story which many country children believed about buzzards? If you see one overhead and you sing out "O Turkey Buzzard, lend me your wing, to fly over the river to see Sallie King," the buzzard will throw up on your head. That's what I believed when I was a child at Dovedale.

———————————

Editor's Note: Originally published as a column in The Macon Telegraph, *Macon, Georgia. Reprinted with permission.*

ROUND ROBIN GIFT
Susan Myrick
1955

Friends of old have heard of the boudoir cap that circulated in my family; those who know me well have heard about the cap so many times they know the story as well as I do, but I hope there are some who don't mind a brief recapitulation of the old tale.

Somebody gave a lavender ribbon and cream lace boudoir cap to one of my sisters, back in about 1923, and she, thinking a boudoir cap a funny sort of thing, sent it on to a second sister; from her it went to a third and so on, until it passed on to nieces and new-brides-in-the-family and wandered as a gift from Hawaii to Oregon to Florida, to Virginia, back to Georgia and off to New York.

Then came misfortune; the cap burned in a fire which destroyed a house belonging to a member of our family.

Which brings me to the point of this story.

Came Christmas, 1955, and I was spending Christmas Eve and Christmas Day with my sister, who clings to the family custom of opening one present the night before Christmas, saving everything else for the following morning.

With much giggling, my nieces selected a gaily wrapped package and insisted that was the one I should open. The card on it suggested the gift might take the place of one gone forever from circulation. I tore off the ribbons and the wrappings and my wondering eyes fell upon a dainty garment of embroidered nainsook.

It was a corset cover! Not a camisole, mind you; it antedated the camisole by some years. Not being an authority on fashions, I can't say what year we left off corset covers and started wearing camisoles; it was about the same time that Teddy bears became fashionable, I guess and Billy Burke pajamas.

My present was handmade, every stitch sewn with patient, skilled fingers. The top of the garment and the armholes were scalloped by hand and the embroidery was as beautiful as if it were made in a French convent.

Where on earth did the thing come from, I wanted to know.

Well, it seems my sister had an old trunk, stored in an old house in the back yard and she was looking for something in it when her daughter found the corset cover and demanded to know what it was.

"A corset cover," her mother said.

"What's a corset cover, Mother?" my niece said, causing her mother to feel aged indeed that she recognized the ancient type of lady's wearing apparel.

So they decided to give the garment to me, hoping it might take the place of the lost boudoir cap. The new round robin gift will soon be on its way to a member of the family—a birthday present to cause idiotic laughter in another household.

———————————

Editor's Note*: Originally printed as a column in* The Macon Telegraph, *Macon, Georgia, December 1955. Reprinted with permission.*

CRIMINALS AND THE COURTHOUSE
Lillas Myrick Lindsley
Circa 1955

MOTHER'S DAY GIFTS

Sometimes, but not always, when the law is broken there is a trial. Someone stole several pieces of porcelain from us, including two antique pieces which cost about $1,500.00. The sheriff, his fingerprint man and the GBI agent were most co-operative in helping to find the thief. The sheriff spent all of three days following different clues and checking to see if a suspected Negro was telling the truth as to his action on the day the porcelains disappeared.

After three days, the local radio in the daily news told of the event and described the articles in detail. To our delight, the most valued articles were returned—by three teenaged boys who rode up on motor bikes and admitted to having taken the items. They wanted them for Mother's Day gifts.

Since the parents were outstanding members of the community and also because we were so delighted to get the porcelains back, we did not have the boys arrested even though a few items of small value were not returned.

We did pay the Negro who was held in jail for a day and night the wages he would have received if he had been at work.

A CASE OF DISCRIMINATION

At one time I had been to court as "a party of the first part," being sued for damages my cows had supposedly done to my neighbor's oats.

I knew, however, that I'd win my suit, for a friend had told me of the time he served on the jury in a similar suit. When the jury retired, someone brought out the fact that the man being sued had lived in the community all his life; the one bringing the suit only 15 years. And with no consideration of evidence the old timer was exonerated.

I am an old timer. Not only was I born in this county and lived here all my life, but my family has been here since 1782, when my great-great-grandfather, as a Revolutionary soldier, received a land lottery grant in this county.

My grandfather bought adjoining land with Confederate money

and on this land I lived until the age of 10. After my father's death we had to leave the farm and move into town because of a law that forbade a woman with only girls to stay in the country. At the time, the population of Milledgeville seemed as small as that of our section of the county, where everyone also knew each other.

We left the horses and buggy but took a cow with us. The four boys who lived next door did the milking on shares. There were no paved sidewalks and few street lights. The houses in town had no bathrooms—but we had left a wooden frame house with an inside bath furnished with plenty of water by a hydraulic ram.

By contrast, the neighbor who brought the suit against me was a newcomer, having lived in the community for less than 20 years.

At the trial one of the man's witnesses was another neighbor.

Most of the first day was spent striking the jury. We were given a list of men (only white men, and no women), and the lawyer for the defense and the lawyer for the plaintiff took turns striking off names until only 12 names were left, the idea being to remove anyone who might be friendly to the other side, or might hold out for a mistrial.

One of the plaintiff's witnesses (who at the time taught my daughters at Sunday school) claimed that the oats would have made a certain number of bushels to the acre if they had not been destroyed by cows. Another witness was another of my neighbors.

I admitted that my cows had gotten out, but through a fence built by the county. In the name of progress and at the county's request, I had given 25 acres of land to the county to widen the road through my place. In return, the county was to move the fence 20 feet back and erect a strong one to hold the cattle. But the fence the county put up along the road right-of-way about five miles would not keep the cows in. I had repeatedly asked the county to fulfill their obligations and put up a suitable fence.

But I did not admit that my cows had done the great amount of damage claimed.

They couldn't have, because at the time in question, the oats were just beginning to sprout, and they came up only sparingly because of the drought throughout all the state. There couldn't have been the bumper crop of oats claimed in the suit.

Apparently a woman being an old timer in the community counted only half as much as it would have for a man—I had to pay half the amount claimed.

A NOT GUILTY VERDICT

I had one experience in court of a trial without a jury. Some Negroes were shooting rabbits along the new road near my house. My daughter, riding horseback on our land, had a narrow escape from getting shot. When we heard the shots fired, we rushed to the scene. By getting the license number of the car parked nearby we were able to get the Negroes accused and taken to trial. The trial was very short; the Negroes admitted the shootings but were allowed to go free—the Georgia law says "one may shoot from the right of way between sunup and sundown."

———————

Editor's Note: The law has since been changed, as a direct result of the efforts of the Lindsley family.

Editress Lizzie Lynn: Or Who Started All This?
Susan Myrick
1960

It is almost impossible, these days, to scan the pages of a woman's magazine or those of the woman's section of a newspaper without finding an article on child-rearing, and there is scarcely a woman who does not read, sometimes eagerly, sometimes wearily, the advice of a child psychologist on how to cope with such problems as bed-wetting, the older child's jealousy of the younger sibling, how to get the youngsters to bed before the late show comes on, what to do about the blue-jeans-sloppy-shirt vogue or how to get the teen-ager off the telephone—in short, how to bring up a healthy, smart, loveable offspring the while you give him plenty of freedom and save him from an Oedipus complex and maybe the juvenile court. It was only a few days ago I found out such articles are not new.

Rummaging around in the old files at the newspaper office where I work, I found a magazine, published in Montgomery, Alabama, in 1860, called *The American Cotton Planter and The Soil of the South.* Like farm magazines of today, it devoted a section to the distaff side, and it contained many columns on how to bring up your child.

The Ladies Department, under the direction of Editress Lizzie Lynn, invites correspondents to send in manuscripts, urges them to "write with a bold hand and with less regard for beauty" and to "punctuate the manuscript as it should be printed." Editress Lynn gives over a couple of inches of type to advising the contributors, and then devotes the rest of her space to articles on child-raising, causing me to wonder if the properly-brought-up child should know how to punctuate and how to put practicality above beauty. Lizzie's parents, in such a case, must have been in need of help from a child psychologist, for Lizzie's punctuation, as well as her grammar, leaves much to be desired in the correspondent's copy as well as in her own dissertations.

The leading article in the Ladies Department, titled "Mother, Where Does Your Child Learn to Deceive?", is signed by one with the implausible name, Ecca, who gets down to business in her first sentence: "Is not deceit common to both male and female, old and young? Why is it so?"

Ecca, as a child, had apparently been impressed with the Ninth Commandment; she is definite about the horrors of deceit: "We all know God abhors lying lips and we'd rather follow our child to its cold grave than have it become a liar," she writes. "I never noticed eight years ago there was so much lying among children but since that time I have been a teacher and had every opportunity to study the character of children placed under my care. Do not be angry, mother, when I say verily I believe it is from you the child gets their (*sic*) first lessons in the hateful and sinful practice. But I think if you can be patient with me I can make it plain to you that your child acquires their first lesson from you."

Ecca, in order to make it plain, illustrates her point with the Jones family who provide the ultimate in how not to bring up a child, and show clearly what Ecca means about the child's lessons in the hateful and sinful practice.

The scene is the Joneses' living room, where Mrs. Jones beside a cozy fire is endeavoring to get her "babe, a bright girl of two summers, to go to sleep." Mrs. Jones is at the same time trying to carry on a conversation with Mr. Jones, and Alice, the bright babe, keeps interrupting. What was of such import that the parents just had to talk about it while poor Alice was trying to go to sleep, Ecca does not reveal. The price of cotton, maybe; the coming of secession, the licking of the Yankees with corn stalks, the latest debate between Douglas and Lincoln? Certain it is the talk was not about the way to train your child, for, as Alice keeps sticking in her two cents' worth, Mrs. Jones applies a smart slap to the infant rear and cries out: "Go to sleep, Alice. Go to sleep or I'll wear you out."

Alice, bright enough at two summers to know Mamma is not really going to wear her out, slips from the arms of her mother and, vowing she wants to "pway peep-eye," trots over to Brother Henry, and the two begin a happy, though noisy, game.

"Henry, if you don't let Alice alone and let her go to sleep, I'll give you a hundred lashes," declares the exasperated Mrs. Jones, scaring the daylights out of Henry, who seems not to be so bright as his sister. Off the two go to the bedroom, leaving Mamma and Papa to their talk. But the noise from the bedroom grows louder and louder as Henry and Alice "merrily jump from one bed to the other," and this time Mr. Jones takes over. He shouts:

"Henry, if you don't let Alice alone and let her go to bed I'll make you sit up all night, ALONE." (The caps belong to Ecca, not to me.)

Squashed by papa's threat, Henry quiets down; not so Baby Alice, who goes on with her merry frolicking until her mother calls out:

"Alice, lie down. Don't you hear that bear coming to get you?" and to add to the fright Mamma "begins to make noises like a bear." The Babe is not bright enough to see through this ruse and she shuts up, leaving her parents to a momentary quiet and an opportunity to go on with their tiresome talk. But peace reigns only briefly. Poor Henry, who has fallen asleep, begins to wail piteously and in a loud voice, "Mamma, don't whip me. I'll be good."

Here, abruptly, Ecca leaves the situation. I don't know how the Joneses coped with that mess. Ecca takes a deep breath and begins a lecture to Mr. and Mrs. Jones and all other parents within the sound of the voice of *The American Cotton Planter and the Soil of the South.*

"Poor Henry," Ecca mourns. "Poor Henry lies dreaming of your threatening punishment. Does not your conscience reproach you? You say your child doesn't mind, now, but as soon as they (*sic*) are capable of distinguishing right from wrong they will soon see that you have been lying and deceiving them.

"Think on what you have done. Would it not be better to draw your child to you by cords of love and then teach them (*sic*) it is their duty to obey you and you will soon find you will take pleasure in them."

She concludes her several-thousand word discourse with the admonition: "Let us all speak kindly to our little ones."

I am puzzled by the situation in the Jones family. The magazine was published in Alabama, a Deep South state, in 1860. Where, I wonder, was Mammy? Have I been misled during all these years when I've been thinking a loving Mammy, in bandanna and a clean cotton dress, was always on hand to teach manners to children and take over when it was time for Babes to be put to sleep? Could it be (I shudder at the thought) that Ecca was really a Yankee who knew no more of Southern customs that she knew of pronouns' antecedents, and who thought Southern White Ladies took care of their own children without any tender aid from Mammy?

Well, Editress Lizzie Lynn accepted the piece from Ecca. Why should I shudder over it? Lizzie, herself, is no mean lecturer on child rearing. Perhaps horrified by Ecca's story of lying lips, the editress gives her views in some two thousand words, and not to be outdone by Ecca, she illustrates with a story about a mother who, though not a woman of lying lips, is nevertheless one who would probably flunk her child psychology course today.

"A little girl was sitting on a stool by the side of her mother," Lizzie says. "The child was busily intent upon threading a large needle. At last, after many ineffectual attempts she succeeded in accomplishing what in her eyes was a difficult feat. Her little face flushed with joy and she exclaimed:

"Look, Mamma. Me shreaded dis needle."

Does Mamma give her offspring a kiss of approval? Does Mamma even say, "Yes, dear?" No. This mother-in-the-form-of-a-fiend says crossly: "Go away and don't trouble me."

The Editress then closes her piece with a bit of advice to parents: "Sympathize with the child's pleasure and their pains and their amusements, labors and disappointments."

Maybe Lizzie was overcome by writer's cramps. Anyhow, the six inches of space she left were filled up by another somebody who called herself Aunt Kizzie, who gave HER notions on child training.

I suppose the War Between the States put an end to *The American Cotton Planter*, and Editress Lizzie Lynn lost her job. I wonder what became of her. Was she, perhaps, in private life a Mrs. Somebody, the mother of seven children, and did they all grow up to be child psychologists who perpetuated the advice-to-parents columns which beset us still?

_____

Editor's Note: Originally published: The Georgia Review, *Vol. XIV, No. 3, Fall 1960, pp.292-295.*

TWO OLD COOKBOOKS
Susan Myrick
1958

In 1870 Bieglow, Thompson, and Brown of Boston published a cookbook called *The Young Housekeeper's Friend*. It was written by a Vermont woman, who, with a fine disregard for identifying initials, called herself Mrs. Cornelius. She showed, too, a fine disregard for accurate measurements: "Take a beer quart of liquid," or "a large handful of flour, or "a little molasses," or "a large spoonful of sugar," various recipes read.

Rent with compassion for the young bride "entering upon the duties of married life, perplexed and prematurely careworn," Mrs. Cornelius packed the pages of her opus with advice which has caused me to be both perplexed and careworn. Since her book fell into my hands I have thumbed through the pages devoted to home nursing, child care, laundry instructions, how to manage a maid and how to get along without one.

My life has been further complicated of late by the acquisition of a second book, *The Dixie Cook Book*, published in 1885 by L. A. Clarkson of Atlanta. The recipes here, the preface says, are "compiled from the treasured collections of many generations of noted housekeepers—tested recipes of the more modern Southern dishes, largely contributed by well-known ladies of the South." In this, as in *The Young Housekeeper's Friend*, only about half the book is devoted to recipes; the other 200-odd pages are concerned with the arts of the toilet, care of babies, what to do about accidents, and home remedies.

The two books vary in the approach. Mrs. Cornelius makes it clear that "good housekeeping is compatible with intellectual culture," and she adds gloomily, "the dearest affections may be chilled through poor housekeeping." Warningly she croaks:

"How often do we see the happiness of a husband abridged by the absence of will, neatness, and economy in the wife? There are numerous instances of worthy merchants and mechanics whose efforts are paralyzed and their hopes chilled by the total failure of a wife in her sphere of duty, and who seek solace in the wine-party or the late convivial supper."

The Dixie Cook Book speaks not of the solace-seeking husband who is wine-bibbing nor of the relation of intellectual culture to housekeeping, but the book is strong on economy and neatness and household care. A four-page dissertation on making butter begins: "No sloven can make good butter. The one thing to keep in mind in neatness, neatness, neatness."

As to economy, *The Dixie Cook Book* at times gives advice which borders on miserliness. Take care of the clothes you have and don't go wasting money on new ones is the burden of some ten pages devoted to ladies' dresses.

"People who are not rich cannot afford to be careless," the housewife is told, and "clothes that are not taken care of will not last as long as those that are kept in order."

When the time comes to buy a new dress (presumably the taken-care-of frock does wear out eventually) *The Dixie Cook Book* tells you:

"Among points to be considered in the selection of a winter dress is its possibility for turning upside down and wrong side out, when its future destiny demands transformation."

Dyeing the material, recutting it, and upsidedowning it when you take care of the frock's future destiny, get some ten pages of discussion.

Mrs. Cornelius, true to her New England nature, also lets drop hints on economy, as when she tells you how to make rose butter. "Gather every morning the petals of the roses that blossomed the day before and put them into a nice stone crock, alternating with the best salt. When all of the petals have been gathered and salted away, put a pound of fresh butter in the top of the jar." Thus you have, she points out, a "good way of obtaining the flavor of roses without expense."

Economy is fine, Mrs. Cornelius thinks, but she warns against parsimony: "The writer has heard of a lady who furnished only two dish towels, fearing that a more ample supply would lead to waste. In one instance, when a superb dinner was served to a large party, the cook was reduced to tearing up a sheet to wipe the dishes."

Catastrophes in the home of the young housekeeper in Mrs. Cornelius' day were legion; there is the one, the author reports, who "had the misfortune to have rats eat up five or six hams," and another who "laid forty yards of the finest Russian linen on the snow to whiten and forgot it until it was reduced to a pulp fit only for the paper mills."

It is a good economy, Mrs. Cornelius tells the young housekeeper, to buy a whole quarter of beef and pack the pieces in a barrel of snow and set it where it will not melt. Snow in New England is to be expected, but snow even in Dixie enters the scene when compilers of *The Dixie Cook Book*, in a section devoted to care of children, advise: "Eating snow, except in limited quantities, is very injurious, producing catarrh, congestion, and other troubles."

Jumping the rope is likewise injurious, you are told. "It is also dangerous. It often results in diseases of the spine and brain."

The Dixie Cook Book's section on medical hints, child care, the infant, and home nursing is a compilation of such vast extent, I wonder how the doctor of 1885 ever had enough patients to enable him to make a living. If your child coughs at night, "boil the strength of a dime's worth of Seneca root in soft water; strain; boil down to one pint and add a cupful of powdered sugar. Give one teaspoon before going to bed" (before who goes to bed, one is left to ponder). If your child has earache: "Roast onions in ashes until done. Wrap them in a strong cloth and squeeze out the juice. To three parts of the juice, add one part laudanum and one part sweet oil. Wash out the ears with warm water and drop a few drops in each ear."

It's a wonder any infant is alive, today, if you believe *The Dixie Cook Book*: "Feather pillows are death to infants; make them of hair or straw."

What ailment do you have in your home? Colds? Use hot penny royal. Stiff joints? "Oil made by tying up the common angle worn is excellent." Tapeworms? "Refrain from supper and breakfast, and at eight o'clock take one-third of 200 minced pumpkin seeds, the shells of which have been removed with hot water; at nine o'clock, take another third, and at ten, the remainder; follow at eleven with a strong dose of castor oil."

In the event you have ambitions toward the speaker's platform, you'll find *The Dixie Cook Book*'s recommendation interesting: "A quart of tar stirred in a gallon of hot water, and a tumblerful taken four times a day, an hour or two after meals, will give greater ease in public speaking."

One supposes gentlemen preferred plump ladies in the eighties; there is a fine dissertation on how to overcome "leanness," which is "caused by lack of power in the digestive organs." While most ladies of today are working to acquire leanness, there may be one or two of you who would like to know how to overcome it. "First, restore digestion, take plenty of sleep, drink all the water the stomach will bear upon arising, take moderate exercise in the open air, eat oatmeal, cracked wheat, baked sweet apples, and cultivate jolly people and bathe daily."

Lean or plump, the housewife of the nineteenth century had to look after laundry, whether she lived in Dixie or in Vermont; both cookbooks advise the young housekeeper to have a light midday meal on wash day, and both tell you how to wash woolens, laces, and delicate prints that are likely to fade. (For this last, "go to the butcher's and buy a pint of fresh beef's gall. Cork it tightly and add a little to the water when washing any article likely to fade. When the bottle is empty or goes stale, get fresh.") And for ease in ironing and polishing shirt bosoms, the housewife simply *had* to have a bosom board. If a husband refused to buy his wife such a household luxury, the wife is to "cut off his supply of hash and sausages, and then take severer means afterward if necessary."

As for the recipes in the two books, if you can figure out the difference between a teacupful, a coffee cupful, a large cupful, and a cupful; if you know how to take a small spoonful of sugar and how much is a handful of flour or a rather large piece of butter; if you have a measure that will tell you how much is about half an ounce of butter or a little essence, you may start cooking. How about making a dish of calf's foot jelly? It seems that everybody took a dish of calf's foot jelly when she went to call on a sick friend.

First, you "clean the calf's feet nicely"; then you put them into five quarts of water and boil until "half the water is wasted away." Then you strain the stuff and set it away until the next morning (you can see this is no dish to whip up when unexpected company arrives half an hour before dinner time), when you skim off the fat, and remove the jelly, being careful not to disturb the sediment. Then you put the jelly into a sauce pan with wine, sugar, and lemon juice and rind "to taste." (Don't be hurrying, yet, to take the jelly to a sick friend; you are not finished with the project.) Now you beat the shells and the whites of five eggs and stir them into the jelly and set the whole business "on the coals." But do not stir it after it begins to warm. Let it boil for about twenty minutes; set off the pan and "let it stand for close to half an hour." It will thus be "so clear you will not have to strain the jelly but once." There the recipe ends. I don't know what you do with the jelly after you have strained it once.

Recipes for cooking wildfowl are many in the two books, but the advice I like best is that T*he Dixie Cook Book* gives on how to catch the fowl alive. "Soak some grain in strong whiskey, scatter it where the fowls are likely to be and take them while drunk."

I hope I shall never have to make a cake frosting by the recipe some unknown Southern lady gave to *The Dixie Cook Book*, but if I ever do, I'll use a pound of the "nicest white sugar," the whites of three "fresh eggs," a teaspoon of the "nicest white starch" pounded and sifted through a piece of muslin, the juice of half a lemon, and a "few drops of essence." I'll put a cork on the tines of a fork and beat the whites to a stiff froth and add them to the sugar. I'll "stir and beat steadily until it will stay where it is put;" it may take me "two hours, perhaps more," the book says, but when I've got it to stay where I put it, I'll dredge the top of the cake with flour, wipe it off with a "clean feather," and put on the frosting.

I hope it will stay where it is put.

––––––––––––

Editor's Note: *Originally published*: The Georgia Review, *Vol. XII, No. 3, Fall 1958, pp 273-277.*

OUR SHERMAN
Lillas S. Myrick Lindsley
1963

When I was a pre-teen on my father's 1000-acre plantation, purchased at nineteen Confederate dollars per acre, Sherman was a one-horse tenant on our plantation. Needless to say, he was born shortly after the general marched to the sea and left freedom behind him, but, free or not, young Sherman's parents had chosen to remain at Dovedale, to continue with their prewar chores for their "Marse Jimmy."

As a boy, Sherman had his own responsibilities as house and yard boy; spring and summer he picked the garden vegetables, everything from sweet potatoes to artichokes and asparagus, and gathered fruits by scampering up the fig and cherry trees or the scuppernong arbors—fruits and vegetables not only for the table but for canning and preserving to be used throughout the winter.

Fall found him gathering the nuts—pecans, walnuts, and scallybarks—as they fell or, one of his favorite chores, climbing high into the trees to bounce on the limbs and shake the fruit down. His winter chores were keeping the eight fireplaces of the plantation house supplied with wood and lit'erd.

When Sherman was older, he had the job of carrying the mail for my mother, postmaster of the Dovedale Post Office. The post office was a one-room house in the side yard, and also served as a general store, carrying flour, sugar, and Arbuckle coffee, the few food necessities that country people bought.

Each morning the mail was put into a bag to be carried to the Meriwether post office, six miles away at the railroad. As he passed each house along the way he picked up the individual mail sack from the gate post.

He placed all the outgoing mail into the Dovedale bag. At Meriwether Station, when the train came by, the Dovedale mail bag went onto the train and the incoming mail bag was thrown off. He distributed sorted mail into his sacks to be left in place on his return, the larger sack for Dovedale. People who lived beyond Dovedale drove their teams over to get their mail. Sherman drove the buggy most of the time, but often winter rains caused such deep ruts in the narrow red road that he was forced to go on horseback.

When Sherman married, he had saved enough money for a down payment on a mule, and Marse Jimmy rented him a farm, a bale of cotton to be paid yearly for rent. The rent included the house for his family, 30 acres of cultivated land, pasture for his mule and cow, and a garden plot, and all the wood he could cut.

In later years, with cotton bringing only 5 cents per pound, the rent changed to $50.00 per year.

In 1933 I had owned the farm where Sherman lived for a number of years; my father was dead; Sherman was 67 years old, his children grown and moved to town. He and his wife lived alone. Cotton prices dropped again, and Sherman not only could not pay his rent, he could not repay the money borrowed for his crop and had no money for feed or fertilizer for another year. He had not raised enough corn to feed his mule through the fall and winter.

Since they were in such bad shaped financially and too old for hard farm labor, and since they had been with us since slavery times, I gave them permission to live on in the house and patch any amount of land that they needed without rent or payment of any kind. They gave their mule to pay for the bad run they had had. A neighbor some five miles away rode over and plowed the land, and then Sherman, with Mamie's help, worked it with a hoe. Their patch included a garden, which most of the year round contained turnip greens, collard greens or cabbage; they also raised sweet potatoes and corn that was carried to the mill only a mile away. They stayed at Dovedale as long as Mamie lived, and then Sherman went to live with one of his children and we never saw him again.

The land was left to grow up in pines.

In 1961 there was no longer a Dovedale Post Office; the Dovedale plantation was still in the family except for a small portion flooded by the Georgia Power Company's Sinclair Dam. Although none of my family lived at Dovedale, I was living on a nearby cattle farm with my family.

When my husband had a dislocated shoulder, I was forced to take over some of his duties, including driving a couple of miles each morning to get Emanuel, a Negro man who put out hay and feed for the cows at various places. Emanuel, like Sherman, rents a one-horse farm from us, and he helps us with fences and feeding during winter months when not busy with his own crops, or during planting season when it is too wet to plow. He does the only actual farming, that is, planting cotton, on the 2500-acre plantation. The other ten tenant houses, once centers of similar farms, have been deserted since the Great Depression and the days of the Public Works Administration. The cotton fields, like those of Dovedale, have grown up in pines or been turned into pastures.

One cold morning while waiting for Emanuel at one of the feeding places, with the motor still running, I got out of the car to scrape the accumulating ice from the windshield. A new car drove by, stopped, backed up; the young Negro woman asked if I were having trouble and could she help. I thanked her and explained that I was waiting for Emanuel. We chatted; I asked her why she was out so early on such a miserable morning, hoping that her answer would tell me who was being so kind and thoughtful. She said that she taught school over town and had not received the radio message that school was closed because of the ice storm. She was returning home.

As she drove off, Emanuel came back to the car. I asked if he know who she was.

"Lawd, Miz Lilla, don't you know her? Dat's Sherman's granddaughter."

WHATEVER BECAME OF THE PROM PARTY?
Susan Myrick
1968

In the early nineteen hundreds it was the most popular form of entertainment for the young people in villages and towns and small cities of the Deep South. In New England or the Midwest a prom meant a dance, but in Dixie the prom was what its name implies, couples promenaded. They walked or strolled around the block, up the street, down the sidewalks, for about fifteen minutes; then they changed partners and walked some more. And there was no handholding—at least not while the pair was in sight of the chaperones. Between proms, the couples regaled themselves with lemonade from a large cutglass punch bowl buried in Dorothy Perkins roses on the broad veranda of the hostess' home.

Today's high school seniors with their Watusi-ing, Frugging, Jerking and Rock-and-rolling will scarcely believe the sort of parties Mama and Grandma went to when THEY were high school seniors—or even after they had been graduated. There was no beer, no nipping, no combo with wild music—just promenading and drinking lemonade, with home-churned ice cream at the "refreshment prom."

As belle of the 1910 prom, Grandma wore her hair in a pompadour, carefully built up over an old stocking or maybe a "store-bought rat"; her evening dress was elaborately tucked and ruffled, with feather stitching between the tucks, and her skirts swept the floor. Rosebuds and ribbons ornamented her bodice, which was modestly high of neckline. A gown cut "too low" was built up with a bit of tulle tucked demurely into the bodice to preclude any glimpse of the divide. Grandma's beaus wore "ice cream britches" (white or cream-colored flannels) with navy blue jackets.

The hostess greeted her guests, gave each one a prom card, a decorated bit of pasteboard folded down the middle. Opened, it revealed twelve numbered lines for writing down the prom partners' names. Tied to the card by a bright ribbon was a tiny pencil, red or blue or green, to match the major color of the picture on the front of the card. The card duly filled out was a status symbol of the day for the girls who took the cards home and stuck them to the wall in a spot next to the passé-partout-framed picture of the best beau. Status was at its highest when the prom card showed three or four proms in a row with the same boy.

"Lawdy, what if Tom asks for three proms in a row and, after I give them to him, Dave asks for three. I'll just die if I haven't got these together to give Dave. But suppose I refuse them to Tom and then Dave doesn't ask." Such an agonizing thought spoiled the evening for many a girl. Sitting out the prom was the worst possible form of wallflower misery. You sat in the porch swing along with a couple of other unlucky girls, or you hung around the punch bowl, slowing dying of embarrassment. The hostess's mother, assisted by Cousin Fannie Lou or Aunt Sallie Fannie, tried to ease your pain by providing tables and games, but everybody knew you hated games and you would rather prom with the pimply-est boy in town than sit out a prom.

When time enough for filling out the cards had elapsed, the hostess rang a little silver bell to signify the start of number one prom, and the boys and girls paired off and started walking. The couples were expected to stay within sound of the bell and return to the front porch when the bell rang at the end of more-or-less fifteen minutes to indicate time to change partners for the next prom. Neighbors sitting on THEIR front porches kept eyes on the prommers, whispered about Lottie Bell's promming four times with Beauregard, or commented on Mattie Sue's extra large hair ribbon, or that visiting girl from Atlanta whose dress was too low; and if couples wandered afar to unlighted streets and dark spots, the girl was promptly labeled "fast" and mothers warned their youngest daughters that she would come to no good end. The nefarious purpose of the young man in the case was only hinted at, but the younger daughters, even in 1912, knew pretty well why the couple liked the darker street.

The prom, preferred over the party where the guests played Rook, Flinch or Dominoes, held on until the days shortly after World War I when the speakeasy, the hip flask, the Bunny Hug, the Charleston, and other sophisticated forms of entertainment occupied the time of eighteen-year-olds and their elders. They were through with such staid goings-on as promming. But proms themselves were not dead; the younger set took them on. It became the proper thing to have a prom party to celebrate your finishing up the seven years of elementary education. A sure sign of summer's approach was not the wearing of white shoes or the swapping of the navy blue woolen blouse you'd been wearing for a white middy blouse, but the items in the social calendar: "Little Miss Harriett Hansom will entertain at a prom party Friday evening at 7:30, inviting members of her class of the seventh grade at Whittle School." Or "Five seventh graders of the Burke School plan a Prom Party"; for promming grew so popular that there weren't enough weekend nights in the spring and summer for each seventh grader to give a party.

"I remember when I was a seventh grader in 1934, I went to twenty-seven prom parties," one Maconite said. "There was one every Friday or Saturday night from mid-May to early September. I had a pink spirit-de-something-or-other evening dress and I wore it to every party and never considered myself one of the disadvantaged."

Little girls who had not long since shed their milk teeth and little boys who had to be coerced into washing faces and combing hair, loved proms. Maybe the boys' thoughts lingered more lovingly on the peanuts, popcorn, potato chips, and punch than on prom cards, but all seventh graders loved proms.

Little girls wore evening dresses; tiny waists were encircled with bright sashes, skirts reached to the ankles, and sleeveless bodices hugged flat bosoms. The only vestige of childhood was the ankle strap, flat-heeled slipper. Flat heels were a great aid when promming began and long skirts were heisted so as not to interfere with a fast walk—or even a run, down the sidewalk. It was not unusual to see a dozen little girls, in evening frocks, chasing a dozen boys down the street for several blocks; when they caught up with the boys, the group hurried back to guzzle punch and fill up on peanuts before the bell rang for the next prom. Boys, who had arrived at the party wearing white trousers, dark coats, newly polished white oxfords, often got home from the party with scuffed shoes and all creases gone from the trousers. Not infrequently, little girls reached home with rents in new frocks, and with ribbon sashes turned into twisted wrinkled things that no amount of pressing could restore, while white organdie frocks were stained green from sitting on the grass.

In the late thirties and early forties prom parties for seventh graders disappeared; just why, nobody seems sure. One Maconite thinks mothers just got so worn out with proms they put a stop to them. A mother from Milledgeville vowed promming got to be such a headache, the evening dress for little girls so costly, that parents laid plans to rid the social world of the prom. Others think the seventh graders got too sophisticated for proms. It is certain that in the mid-forties, the sock-hop became the proper thing for seventh grade girls, and the new status symbol was how dirty your socks were when you got home from the hop. Certain, too, it is that the prom has vanished along with shoe-button hooks, horse-drawn vehicles, the frow, and the quill pen.

Research has failed to reveal who first thought of prom parties or when the first ones were given. Maybe the prom has its roots in religious convictions, still fairly common in the Deep South, which is opposed to dancing, as well as drinking, though this seems strange for Georgia, a state settled by English and Irish who never disapproved of a reel or a jig. Perhaps the conviction that dancing was a sin came to us from our Puritan ancestors who came South from New England to settle. Maybe the idea of dancing as a sin stemmed from the teaching of Methodist John Wesley, though the Baptists disapproved of dancing as much as did the Methodists. Records of some village Baptist church in Georgia tell of the church's action toward certain members guilty of dancing. The church record called the action "withdrawal of fellowship"; the common parlance was "Sister Susie was turned out of the church." It is certain that dancing, card playing, drinking, and gambling were regarded as sins by many church members in the Deep South, though some religious ones, who regarded the round dance as sinful, thought the Virginia Reel or other forms of square dancing, such as Twistification, were not harmful to the morals.

There are those who opine that the prom party was invented by some careful mother in the late nineties when the forces of social decorum had a firmer grip upon young women than they have today. It is debatable whether the relaxed grip of today's mother is due to the youth's taking the bit in his teeth or due to the parents' lingering in bars and doing the Watusi at the Country Club.

Careful mothers in the bigger cities in Georgia, in the days when mothers did no rhumbas, formed no conga chains, and drank nothing stronger than blackberry shrub, encouraged their daughters to attend cotillions. Popular in the period 1879 to 1890, the cotillion carried over into the early nineteen hundreds, according to the recollections of some elderly ladies of the Capital City's fashionable set. The lady wore a formal gown with long white gloves and with a train which she carried in her arm by means of a silken loop. Her escort wore tails and white tie and the pair moved with graceful elegance in time to a march played by the orchestra. Down the center of the room the couples marched;

they separated, the lady going one way and her escort the other; they met again; they repeated the figures in twos and fours and eights and sixteens. Finally, the ladies marched to one side of the room and their partners to the other side, where tables laden with favors awaited them. The gentlemen received knives, papier-mâché figures, tiny barrels of candy. Favors for the ladies were Japanese paper parasols, Japanese fans, feather fans, little ornaments for their hair, pine trays, holders for combings, tiny Japanese lanterns with lighted candles.

Gone from today's parties are cotillions and proms, but since fashions turn in circles (we now have Norfolk Jackets and long-waisted frocks of the ilk of the Twenties), maybe proms will come back as the pendulum swings. I doubt it, however. The world changes, and the youngsters move into realms their parents will never enter. It is doubtful that the sacred will prevail over the secular, and that rural and religious attitudes of our provincial culture will again take over in the South.

Editor's Note: Originally published in The Georgia Review, *Vol. XXII, No. 3, Fall 1968, pp.354-359.*

OLD BETHEL
Allie Myrick Bowden

I was three and one-half months old on April 18, 1896 when I was christened by the Reverend George Griner of Bethel Church. About six years later, I "joined the church." Until I was aged 15, Bethel was the only church in existence for me. I had never seen or heard of any others.

The church was a rectangular one-room wooden building with long green blinds equally spaced on each side to shut out the extreme heat of the sun or the occasional cold of winter. It stood in a grove of large oaks which furnished shade for the carriages, buggies, carts and wagons, and for the horses which had brought their owners to church.

When we arrived for Sunday school or church services, dressed in our best, even my 10-year-old brother wore shoes for this once-a-week occasion.

My father drove the family to the church and put us out of the buggy onto the wide porch that extended across the whole front of the building. Two large doors opened from the porch—one for the women and children and the other for the men and boys over 12 years. From the front wall to the altar, a 3-foot-high wall ran down the middle of the pews to separate the men from the women. I could just see the top of my father's head on his side as I sat beside my mother. About three-fourths of the way to the pulpit (we never heard the word sanctuary) the outer pew of the second row gave way to the organist and to the "amen corner," where the pews ran crosswise.

Beyond the amen corner a small door opened to the outside. Wood for the heater, used only on a few cold Sundays, was brought through this door. Outside the door a winding path led to the spring from which was brought water for christenings and to provide a drink for the minister during his long sermon.

Across the three rows was a long seat where the members sat to be confirmed or to await their turn for taking communion.

The church was (and still is) located in northwest Baldwin County in the country not far from Meriwether Rail station of a local line of the Central of Georgia Railroad, and about eight miles from the town of

Milledgeville. Members came from the homes within about five miles from Meriwether Station.

When I attended, the church was called "Old Bethel Church" because it had stood there since 1853; it replaced an earlier church built about 1813. The land probably belonged to the Hughes family.

———————————

Editor's Note: Meriwether Station has been closed for many years although the rail line is still open; it is used now only to carry coal to Plant Branch of the Georgia Power Company. The road from the Station to the Church is now closed, flooded by the waters of Lake Sinclair. John and Amy Myrick gave land for the church, but there was no deed until Samuel Hughes deeded it in 1872. See Appendix IV for more information on Bethel Church.

AUNT LIZZIE GOOD
Susan Myrick
1977

My Aunt Lizzie Good was so called to distinguish her from another Aunt Lizzie, but I did not know that when I was a small child. I though her name was due to her reputation for being a good woman, though I knew vaguely that the name had something to do with the fact that she was the wife of Uncle Good, whose real name was Goodwin Dowdell Myrick.

He was given his grandfather's name, Goodwin, because in our family everybody was always named some family name; thus you would know that Elizabeth Stajarret Myrick was a descendent of a forbearer whose surname was Stajarret and poor Elizabeth might well be glad that was her middle name, no matter how bitterly she resented being called Lizzie or Betsy as the case might be.

Our grandmother was called Lizzie and our sister Elizabeth was called Tippie and there were Beths and Bettys and at least one Betsy; Elizabeth was quite a favorite name for our folks.

Aunt Lizzie Good was really Elizabeth Garrard Hawkins Myrick, but "Aunt Lizzie Good" she was to me, and her Goodness was all church-going goodness, I thought. She never let the doors of Bethel Church (which she fondly spoke of, always, as "Ole Bethel") open without her presence there. Sunday school every Sunday; preaching every third Sunday; prayer meetings every second and fourth Wednesdays, and two weeks of revival services, which she called "protracted meeting," in summer when the crops had been laid by.

Sunday after Sunday, the bay horse was hitched to the "top buggy," and Aunt Lizzie and Uncle Good left their boxwood-bordered yard to drive the three miles to Ole Bethel at 10 a. m. If it were winter time, they would start earlier, for Uncle Good served not only as chief bass singer and amen-corner-sitter and leader in prayer, he served as the janitor. (Although I am sure Aunt Lizzie Good would rise from her grave and haunt me if she knew I called him a janitor.) Uncle Good, nevertheless, made the fire in the pot-bellied stove which stood in the front of the church, winter and summer, and it was Uncle Good who stoked the fire quietly at least once during the service on Sundays.

Some little Negro boy must have brought the wood into the church and stacked it neatly, for I never saw Uncle Good bring in any wood. And I recall one Sunday when I had arrived early for Sunday school when it was bitter cold and Aunt Lizzie was telling Uncle Good, in a masterful tone, he'd have to fetch some more wood for that "no account boy" had evidently not been near the church yard that week.

Uncle Good, who was always smiling through his beard and his luxurious mustache, brought the wood in and urged me closer to the stove with a cheerful, "Here, honey, you look frozen. Let me run your fingers a bit to warm them." But it was only a few minutes I was allowed to warm myself. The handful of neighborhood attendants on the Sunday school were arriving and Aunt Lizzie told Uncle Good, "It looks like Brother Jones will not be here this mawnin. You'd better pick out the songs, Good."

And Uncle Good, always obedient to Aunt Lizzie's command, picked out the hymns and started the morning service. Mrs. Jehu Humphries played the little foot-pumped organ, and the congregation, led by Aunt Lizzie's high soprano voice, sang.

Mrs. Humphries, I remember, was for years the greatest puzzle of my life. I knew that everybody spoke of her as Mrs. Jehu Humphries; they did so to distinguish between her and Mrs. Will and Mrs. Tom Humphries; but to my childish mind, the name, "Jehu," did not exist, in spite of Aunt Lizzie's teaching me my Sunday school lessons as earnestly as she could. The name was "G. Hugh" Humphries to me, for some inexplicable reason, and I used to wonder and wonder why Mrs. G. Hugh Humphries' initials were J. P. H. instead of G. H. H. (I knew what the initials were because Mrs. Humphries' little niece was in the same English grammar class with me when we learned about initials in the third grade.)

Mrs. Humphries would pull out most of the stops on the little organ, always pulling out to its fullest extent the "vox humana" and she'd pump so hard with her tiny feet in their too-tight shoes that the plume on her hat would shiver and tremble in a fashion which fascinated me.

And as Aunt Lizzie Good reached about the fourth or fifth note of the song, her voice, high and full, soaring as the violin obligato soars above the full orchestra, Mrs. Humphries would join in with her alto. When those two voices joined, even the most timid of the congregation dared to raise her voice in song, for no less a voice than that of the most powerful opera singer could have been heard along side Aunt Lizzie's and Mrs. Jehu Humphries' voices.

"I am bound for the promised la-a-a-a-nd,
I am bound for the promised land
Oh, who will come and go with me?
I am bound for the promised land."

The organ boomed and Mrs. Humphries plumes quivered, the congregation sang joyously with their leaders, and Uncle Good might be heard occasionally as he reached a low bass note, singing by ear, as it were, and harmonizing on the places where it was easy.

When we had sung the first, second and fourth verses, omitting the third, as all Methodist groups appeared to do (I used to wonder why anybody troubled to write the third verse), Mrs. Humphries would hold the final note long and quavering but not long enough to outlast Aunt Lizzie Good's final triumphant sound. I am bound to say, however, that Mrs. Humphries played fair and always held a quiet tremolo on the final organ note until Aunt Lizzie was ready to relinquish her last note of song.

We'd sing another hymn and then Uncle Good would lead in prayer, kneeling down in front of the unpainted pine chair with its shuck bottom, the soles of his Sunday shoes turned toward the congregation, and praying earnestly and long for the absent, the sick, the sinful. Aunt Lizzie Good would sound a fervent "Amen" at intervals, impressing me more and more with the idea that her name stemmed from her religious fervor.

Then we'd go to our respective "classes," not that we had any classrooms; we'd retire to certain areas of the church. The adults, usually three or four of them, would sit in the Amen corner for the Bible Class; the young people would arrange themselves in the front pews near the stove; we of the children's class would go over to the benches where Aunt Lizzie sat close to the organ. The mountain went to Mohamed; nobody would have thought of expecting Aunt Lizzie to go to the class instead of having them move over to where she sat.

I can remember little of the Sunday school lessons except the little colored cards which Aunt Lizzie Good gave to each of us, cards which I suspect she bought from her own meager purse with money she got for the yellow butter she sent to town every Friday. The little pasteboards with their shiny surfaces and their pictures of Jesus and the prophets, major and minor, and the apostles and Mary Magdalene, and the healing of Lazarus and the Boy David playing his harp, and the Ark and the animals at the flood time—those cards enchanted me. Their colors were bright and garish perhaps to an artist; to my country-child eyes, they were the most beautiful things in the world, far lovelier even that the calendar which Remington Arms Company sent to Papa, with its pictures of a man in a bright red hunting coat, his gun over his shoulder and a brown and white setter eagerly jumping beside the hunter.

I'd clutch the Sunday school card tightly in my little fist and take it home each Sunday to put with the others in my collection. And, at intervals, while at play, I'd muse on Aunt Lizzie Good and her Goodness.

She did not come often to see us. She lived some two miles from us but she was a busy farm wife, as my own mother was. But now and then she'd drive over for an afternoon, bringing one of her grandchildren to play with the assorted children at our house. For Aunt Lizzie was much older than my mother and her grandchildren were the approximate ages of Mama's younger offspring. Not that Aunt Lizzie looked old; she was erect and she held her head high and she walked briskly. In fact, Aunt Lizzie was brisk about everything.

When she came to see us on an occasional afternoon visit, she and Mama sat on the front porch, each in a rocking chair that had wide arms and broad bottoms. Discussing some phase of life, Aunt Lizzie would slap the arm of the chair with her hand and declare in a loud voice of righteous indignation:

"Thulia, it's wrong!"

And Mama would echo: "It's wrong, Lizzie."

I am certain that neither Mother nor Aunt Lizzie Good ever did anything that they thought was wrong.

———————————

Editor's Note: A book now in the possession of Lindsley Shane Bramlett (grandson of Lillas S. Myrick Lindsley) has the flyleaf inscription that the book was the property of "Elizabeth Stagira Dowdell 1842." She married Stith Parham Myrick.

THE MYRICK GIRLS AT COLLEGE
Allie Myrick Bowden
1981

The first of the Myricks to enter Georgia Normal and Industrial College was Susan, who entered in September, 1907, as a freshman after taking the required entrance examinations. Graduates of accredited high schools entered without examination, but since Susan's previous education had been in a little one-room school on her father's plantation, the examination was required. Susan passed glowingly.

When she replied to the question, "What is your favorite book?" *"David Copperfield* by Charles Dickens, because of its continuing wit and constant pathos," she captured the attention of Mr. Powell, the head of the English department, and he gave her special training and guidance which was largely responsible for her later success as a newspaper columnist and magazine writer.

Susan's unfailing cheerfulness and ready wit made her a favorite of her classmates. She even brought humor to her Latin class, coming to class with such questions as, "What becomes of all the pins we drop?"

"They fall to earth and become *terra* pins."

Susan's home for three and a half years was the second floor of the Mansion, then used as a dormitory, or the Mansion Annex, where, in each case she had three (or was it five?) roommates. Then, when her father died and the family moved to Milledgeville, she and the sisters who followed were "town girls," living at home.

"Town girls" in most respects were subject to the same rules as the dormitory girls. They wore the same brown serge skirts (soon slick in the back), long-sleeved, high-collared white shirtwaists, black ties and brown belts—the belts a necessity to cover the row of safety pins which held skirt and waist together. For church and special occasions, they wore a brown fitted coat suit until spring, when white waists and skirts replaced them. And woe to anyone whose skirt, white or brown, measured more than six (or was it four?) inches from the floor. "Town girls" were under the same restrictions as others as to dating, or even speaking to boys!

During the last half of Susan's senior year, the second sister, Allie, entered the Sub-Freshman class and began a long session of two

Myricks in the College. This time, two as students; the following year (1911-12), one a student and one a faculty member. Later on, there would be two on the faculty, while another sister was a student.

Each year, a few outstanding students from the graduating class were chosen to return to the College for a year as "scholarship teachers." Whether the idea was conceived by Dr. Chappell, the first President, or by Dr. Parks, the second, I do not know, but it must have helped the college budget considerably. For the chosen scholarship teacher was so pleased with the honor and the prospect of a year's experience of teaching in a familiar setting, with excellent supervision, that she happily accepted the small salary of about thirty-five dollars a month. Susan was one of those chosen for this honor, and was assistant to Miss West in the Physical Education Department, an experience which led to a career of teaching physical education for many years.

Allie followed closely in Susan's footsteps. She, too, was well liked by her classmates, as evidenced by the fact that she was elected president of her class in her sophomore year, and continued to hold that position until graduation. When Allie was a senior, Susan, after an absence of three years, was again teaching at the college (Allie attending one of her classes), and Katie, the third sister, was a freshman. The following year, Allie, as Scholarship teacher, and Katie, as a sophomore, represented the family. Katie, differing from her older sisters, chose the Home Economic course which she so loved that, in spite of many battles with Miss Able of the sewing department, after her graduation in 1918, chose to go to the University of Georgia for a degree in Home Economics. (At that time, GN&IC did not confer degrees.)

When Katie was a junior, Lillas, the fourth sister to attend GN&IC, entered as a freshman, and, again, there were two Myricks as students in the College. One of Lillas' favorite stories was to tell how the Myrick sisters made the Glee Club, although, except for Susan, they were almost tone deaf. She said, "Susan made the Glee Club because she really could read notes and had a good voice. Allie, because she was class president. Katie, because Miss Tucker (Musical Director) liked her, and I, because they wanted one good-looking girl in the club!"

Lillas graduated in 1920 but decided to continue her work there as a member of the first class to receive a degree from G.S.C.W. in 1922. In the meantime, Susan had returned to the College as Director of the Physical Education Department (1920-1922); Allie, after graduate work at Columbia University, returned to serve as head of the Psychology Department where she introduced the first courses in Child Psychology and in Intelligence and Educational Tests and Measurement (1921-1923). After her marriage in the summer of 1923 she continued as a part-time faculty member until she and her husband left Milledgeville.

After graduation, Lillas taught intermittently in the Chemistry Department while obtaining her Master's Degree at Columbia University and completing the academic work for her doctorate. She was assistant to Dr. Beeson; when he was made president of the college, she was assistant to Dr. Lindsley, who replaced Dr. Beeson as head of the department.

In 1934, Lillas married Dr. Lindsley. Thereafter, the name of Myrick did not appear on either the faculty roster or the student lists.

Editor's Note: These recollections are excerpts from an article Allie wrote, "A Quarter of a Century at G.N. & I.C. and G.S.C.W. with the Myrick Sisters," published in Columns, Winter, 1981, back cover. Printed with permission.

SHERMAN
Allie Myrick Bowden
April 1989

[Sherman's given name was John Henry Calhoun.]

His graying hair, gentle manners, devotion to children, and, most of all, his name were evidence of his age. He had been born on my grandfather's plantation in middle Georgia which lay in the path of General W. T. Sherman on his famous "March to the Sea" in 1864 and 1865. It was the belief of most slaves who lived within that famous path that it was Sherman, not Lincoln, who gave them their freedom. They honored him by naming their newborn sons "Sherman" for several years thereafter.

In the years 1900-1910, when I was growing up on my father's plantation, Sherman was our house servant. His fellow servants, too, were descendents of the slaves of my grandfather—those slaves who stayed on the plantation from a sense of loyalty or from a realization that at that time their best future lay in staying where they were instead of following the rabble of the Union Army only to be shortly abandoned, hungry and homeless, as they trudged along.

Among the younger children in our family, Sherman was our favorite person. We were scarcely aware of all he did for the family's comfort; he was just a part of our growing up—as much so as going barefoot in summer, turning the handle of the big ice cream freezer on the back porch, picking wild plums, strawberries, dewberries and blackberries in the fields, and wearing balmorals in winter, from December to April first, no matter what the weather. (Balmorals were so named after the wool balmorals of the Scots at Balmoral Castle.)

Sherman's day began at the first cock's crow. He hurried from the small cabin, which my father had built for him, to the house, stopping only at the backyard deep well. There, hand over hand, he pulled the ropes to start the buckets moving, one descending as the other rose. The empty buckets swayed back and forth, hitting the rock walls of the well in many-toned clangs. To Sherman, the sounds were his carillon, his steel band, his morning song or matins. The bucket hit the bottom of the well, then the bucket, "dripping with coolness, rose from the well." (Wordsworth)

Sherman took the gourd which hung from the well post, quaffed a long, cool drink, and was ready for the day. He set the first of many buckets of water to be carried to the house on the water shelf in the back hall where a silver dipper hung—my mother's one insistence on carrying over some evidence of better days.

Then Sherman went to the kitchen to take up yesterday's ashes and start a fire in the enormous iron stove which stood in one corner of the kitchen. First he put crumpled paper, then those wonderful-smelling lit'erd (lightwood) knots from long-dead pine trees, then pine chips, and, finally, the stove-length logs he had cut and brought to the kitchen last evening. As the stove grew hot, Sherman, a bucket in each hand, again and again returned to the well for water to fill the kettles on the stoves, the pitchers in the bedrooms, and buckets for basins on the back porch.

He added more logs to the fire; all was ready then for the cook to prepare breakfast, and such a breakfast! Every day! Not even Tiny Tim's luxurious Christmas dinner could equal it. There was the inevitable dish of hominy grits served with red-eyed gravy or with the rich gravy made from the family's freshly made pork sausage or with freshly churned butter. There was ham, bacon or sausage, eggs— usually scrambled for the children, soft-boiled for Papa, poached for Grandma, and fried for the older adults. Then there were gallons of fresh milk, tea and coffee. Always we had hot biscuits and either waffles or battercakes (pancakes), homemade jam or preserves and Georgia cane syrup, made from blue ribbon cane grown on the farm, far better than molasses or sorghum.

While the family ate breakfast, Sherman was bringing freshly drawn water from the well to refill the kettles and pitchers, taking out ashes from last night's fires in the sitting room or bed rooms, and emptying and cleaning the bed chamber slop buckets. These chores accomplished, Sherman soaped and scrubbed his hands in the basin reserved for his use on the back porch. Now he was ready for *his* breakfast which the cook soon brought to his seat in the corner of the kitchen.

After breakfast, after bringing out the baskets for the children to fill with chips for starting the next day's fires, Sherman went to the wood pile, sharpened the ax at the iron vice and began cutting more logs and kindling. Soon it was: "Papa, can Sherman go with me to get some plums (or strawberries, blackberries, dewberries or scaly barks, a delicacy seldom found outside Georgia)?"

"Soon as he finishes his wood chopping."

"Come on, let's get our buckets!" Four pair of little legs, fat or slim, all tanned almost to the color of Sherman's skin, raced to get his or her own bucket.

"Put on your sun bonnets," Mama called.

Sherman, armed with his heavy cane for any chance snakes, was soon ready and away we went across the fields to gorge on the delicious fruit, and perhaps to cover the bottoms of the buckets. When Lil, aged four, her little mouth red with plum or berry juice, began to falter, Sherman took her in his arms or on his back and we slowly returned home.

Sherman's busy day with its unending chores continued until "first dark" when the wood boxes had to be refilled, water drawn for buckets, kettles and pitchers, the hand basins and the big foot tub on the back porch steps for the grimy hands and feet to be washed before supper. Sherman, tired and stiff in the joints, then ambled to his own outdoor bath and to don clean clothes before galloping back to the kitchen to sit on his chair behind the big stove.

It was a short rest: No sooner was he settled in his chair than in came the children, each scrambling for a place on Sherman's knee or the nearest place to him on the warm, well-scrubbed pine floor.

"No pushing now or ole Brer Wolf will get you."

They quieted down and were soon enthralled by his tales of Brer Fox, Brer Rabbit, Sis Cow, and Miss Meadows and the gals.

Too soon the cook called, "Time for supper." Usually avid for food, the children were reluctant to leave Sherman and his stories. "Just one more tale, Sherman. Please!"

"You scoot along now before your Daddy gets a strap to you."

Sherman would lean back in his chair for a long, well-deserved rest while the family was eating supper and before the cook brought his piled-up plate of luscious and much-appreciated supper.

Thus the days went by until that memorable day of October 8, 1909.

There was a decided chill in the air. Sherman was chopping wood for the coming fires of winter. The children were at school in the little one-room schoolhouse my father had built on one corner of the plantation, to be used by all the children of the neighborhood as well as his own, he and the county dividing the costs of a teacher. Sherman laid his axe down to watch as my father, looking so frail and tired and somehow old, rode in after his daily round of inspecting the farms. He headed straight for the well, dismounted, tossed the reins to Hezekiah and drew up a bucket of cool water. My father took a long, refreshing drink.

Suddenly, he stood still and peered into the bucket. "Sherman, come! Look at the mud in the bottom of the bucket! Tell Hezekiah to go for the well digger and tell him to come the very first day he can to clean out the well. All these heavy rains we have had have washed dirt into the well."

He leaned over to look into the depths of the well, hands braced on the well cover supports, mouth open to breathe more easily. He then stepped back, his countenance a combination of consternation and distress. His false teeth had fallen to the bottom of the well!

Five hundred dollars gone; another five hundred for a new set. It was twelve miles to the nearest dentist, trip after trip in the horse-drawn buggy, weeks of no teeth, discomfort and pain while getting the new set adjusted.

"Sherman, call in the hands. Someone will have to go down and get my teeth. It will take weeks to find the well digger this time of year."

A group soon assembled around the well. The regular buckets and ropes were replaced by the iron chains and man-sized buckets, always kept in the carriage house for emergency.

"Now, who wants to go down?" Complete silence. "Hezekiah?"

"Naw suh, Mr. Myke, I ain't going down no well."

"Will?"

"Naw suh! I'se skeered."

"Tom?"

"It's too cold for me down there, Mr. Myke."

"Well, I'll just go myself. Hezekiah, you are the strongest, you can man the chains. Will, you can stand by to help him with the speed."

My father removed his glasses, pulled on his jacket and put his hand on the big bucket. Sherman walked over:

"You ain't strong enough, Mr. Myke. I'll go."

And into the bucket he climbed; he was lowered straight toward the bottom with no side to side swaying to start the musical clink. A few minutes later Sherman called, "I got 'em, Mr. Myke." And then, "I'm in boys! Pull me up."

"Hallelujah! Here he comes!" The on-lookers were grinning, the bucket was rapidly ascending when, suddenly a sound greater than a big drum could make, louder than a clap of thunder, reached their ears. Chains were jerked from the powerful grip of Hezekiah. Loosened by the weeks of torrential and continuous rains, rocks were falling from the walls to the well bottom, striking Sherman and the big bucket as they fell. Finally the noise receded.

"Sherman, are you there?"

"Yes, sir, but I'm pinned in up to my waist."

"Are you hurt badly?"

"No, sir, but I can't move my legs."

"Keep still and pray. We'll get you out. Come on, men, we've got to dig Sherman out. Tom, go ring the farm bell—we'll need everybody on the place to help."

The big bell clanged; the farm hands and neighbors came running, the women groaning. Hezekiah led the way to the carriage house to find the other man-sized bucket which they attached to the windlass all ready for the rescue. No need to ask for volunteers this time! Every strong man was ready to go down to rescue Sherman on that bright October morning. Many men were needed as one replaced another in the hard work of lifting the heavy rocks into the bucket to be pulled to the surface, emptying the rocks into a rock pile.

Every few minutes my father called, "Sherman, are you all right?" to be answered, cheerfully, "I'se still here!"

But then it was: "Yas sir, but my feet is cold."

"Tom, go to the house and tell Miss Kate to send me a bottle of brandy. We will send it to Sherman when the next bucket goes down."

The day progressed, the pile of rocks lifted from the well grew higher, and the sky began to redden with a sinister glow.

"Hezekiah, take Bill Nye (our speediest horse) and go for the doctor. Somebody get lanterns so we can see what we are doing. Susan, tell your mother to keep a big fire going in the back sitting room and all of you young ones, go to the house and stay in your mother's room until morning."

In the back sitting room, the fire was blazing and the room getting warmer. A mattress was laid on the floor in front of the fire, blankets were warming on the hearth, and kettles of water were steaming nearby on the kitchen stove. The doctor arrived as the evening glow faded and darkness began to cover the land. In the glow of the lanterns, the men worked on until at last Sherman was freed from the rocks and brought to the surface. The doctor stood by as Sherman, no longer talking, eyes closed, was placed on a warm blanket made into a sling and carried into the house where he was placed on the mattress.

The door was closed. The children, tears streaming down their cheeks, stood in their mother's room, listening to every sound and possible word. They heard the doctor say, "He's breathing —keep rubbing his feet—get another blanket—put another hot cloth on his head—try a few drops of whiskey on his lips."
And then, "I think he is going to pull through, if he can stay here for a few days with someone to look after him."

"Of course. And Tom's wife will take care of him."

A few days and Sherman was back in his cabin, a few more days and he was able to hobble up to his chair in the kitchen.

"Here I is, chillun. Ole Brer Rabbit done fool 'em again. And your Daddy's got his teeth. He say I don't never have to draw up no more water nor do any more hard work." Sherman paused, sighed: "But I'll sure miss hearing that good music every day!"

Editor's Note: An article in the Milledgeville, Georgia, The Union-Recorder, *December 26, 1905, reported on the event that instilled so much fear in the farm hands about going down the well. In that time, all farms had wells and all wells were hand dug, so going down into a well was a common event for farming people.*

> *Tom Thomas, a Negro man, was buried in a well at the home of Mr. J. D. Myrick near Dovedale last Wednesday. The Negro went into the well to recover a pair of spectacles which had been dropped into it. In descending he struck the wall causing it to cave in. Thomas was buried beneath the debris, and when gotten out his life was extinct.*

SARA LOU
Allie Myrick Bowden
Circa 1990

Sara Lou's large, strong, muscular hands, arms and shoulders of her fat, erect body were evidence of many years of kneading dough for rolls, biscuits and pie crusts. They spoke, too, of the ease with which she lifted heavy iron frying pans, kettles and lids of the iron cook stove to add another stick of wood to keep the temperature just right.

She walked slowly from stove to table to dishpan. The dishpan sat on a long shelf on the further side of the kitchen beside the "disposal." The disposal was a large opening on the shelf through which dirty dish water, scraps, or chicken entrails were dropped into a huge tub on ground level, walled off from the remaining basement with a gate, through which the tub was pulled onto a wheelbarrow by Hezekiah. He would empty it into the pig trough some distance away.

The kitchen was Sara Lou's domain. No one dared enter it under strict orders, except for just before supper, when the children, hands clean for the evening meal were allowed into "Sherman's corner." We gathered around Sherman, his hands equally cleaned up prior to his own supper, to listen to his wonderful stories of Brer Fox, Brer Rabbit and Sis Cow. At other times, when I could come no further than the kitchen door, Sara Lou would often bring me a baked potato or a tea cake. Was it because I was the smallest, although not the youngest, of the children that she favored me in this way? I was always fragile; evidently Sara Lou thought I needed "fattening up."

As I grew older, I always rushed to the dining room the minute I came from school to see what she had made for us to assuage our hunger before supper. Always there was a large oval white platter, piled with gingerbread cookies or some other tea cakes for our afternoon tea parties. The platter sat above the "safe" in the dining room. This safe was a kind of cupboard. The doors of the upper two-thirds were punched with numerous holes to let in the air for cooling left-over butter; the lower third contained such items as syrup pitchers and opened bottles of pickles, preserves or jam.

Sara Lou had made these snacks for us between times spent picking the feathers of the newly killed chickens, turkeys, guineas or the partridges and the doves which my father or brothers had brought in from their hunting trips, cooking the three meals of the day, scrubbing the floor, and keeping the fire in the stove going just right for the next baking. The kitchen was truly Sara Lou's home from seven a.m. to seven or eight p.m.

Imagine my unhappiness when, for four days, there was no Sara Lou in the kitchen. A strange Negro woman took over. There were no cookies on the sideboard, no hot potatoes sneaked to me, no sitting in Sherman's corner to hear his stories. Then my mother told me that that Sara Lou, who lived in a little house "on the place" with her husband, Alf, had had twin babies and was staying home for a while to take care of them. And she told me that Sara Lou had named the babies Susan and Allie for my older sister and me.

I was jubilant! My mother said she would take us to see the babies soon. Next day, she took Susan and me with her in the carriage into town, which was twelve miles away. Our favorite horses, Bill Nye and Lady, pulled the buggy. In town, we went immediately to the dry goods store to purchase two little white baby caps, all lace and ribbons, for our namesakes. Next day, we walked with Mama to Sara Lou's house (we were never allowed to go to a servant's house alone), to take the presents to the little girls. Sara Lou tied the caps under their chins. I was rapturous; the little black faces in the pretty lace caps were more beautiful than any thing I had ever seen. Susan was the larger of the two and Allie was quite fragile, but Sara Lou promised that next time she would let us hold the babies *very carefully*.

Sara Lou was soon back in the kitchen and the world resumed its usual life for several months with Jennie Tuft's taking care of the babies. We would see them now and then when she rode them in the little baby carriage my father and mother bought for them. With Sara Lou back in the kitchen, fried chicken tasted better, waffles and bacon were crisper, grits were fluffier and tea cakes were more abundant.

Little Susan continued stouter and stronger each day; little Allie more fragile. It was but a few months after the birth of the twins that Sara Lou took me in her arms and told me that little Allie had died. It was the first tragedy and, in a way, the most lasting tragedy of my life.

Many years later, when I was nearly grown and living with my mother and younger sister in town, where we had moved after my father's death, there came a knock at the front door. I went to answer it. There stood a very black, well-dressed woman.

"Is this where Miss Kate Myrick lives now?"

Before I could answer, my mother was at the door: "Who? Oh, Sara Lou! Where did you come from after so many years? I thought you were in Detroit! Come in! Come in! I'm so glad to see you." They walked into the living room and then followed much excited talk.

"Now when were you with us, Sara Lou? I know you cooked a thousand wonderful meals for us when we lived in the country."

"Yes'm, Miss Kate. I cooked for you and Mr. Myrick from the time Miss Susan was your lap baby and Miss Allie was your tiny baby till Mr. Myrick died and I went to Detroit."

There followed much talk of her years in Detroit and manner of life as a widow. We were so glad she had hunted us down when she came back to Georgia in the 1920's. She rejoiced that Miss Susan was still a happy, healthy young woman and that Miss Allie, though still very fragile, was to be married in a few months.

Editor's Note: At the beginning of this manuscript, the author lists those people she would like to write about: Sherman, Sara Lou, Jennie Tuft & Alf, Will Collier, Robert Liptrot, Hezekiah Freeman and Lugene Tuft. The only accounts she finished were this and "Sherman."

Who Shall Gather Them
(A Short Story)
Susan Myrick
Circa 1960

We brought nothing into this world and it is certain we can take nothing out. The Lord gave and the Lord hath taken away; blessed be the name of the Lord.

Eighty-five-year-old Mrs. Blasingame, sitting in the front row of chairs in the undertaker's parlor, sniffed at the sick-sweet smell of cape jasmine and roses and carnations, and half rose in her chair the better to see the body of Jim Horley lying in the open coffin, his white beard free of tobacco stains for the first time in many years, his white shirt and blue serge coat immaculate. She wondered if the undertaker had put a tie on Jim—she couldn't see it poking out from under that beard. She looked around the room to see if she could recognize any members of Jim's family. She had know his parents and his sisters and brothers and she knew the cousins who lived in Burnsville, but the visiting nephews and nieces who had come to the funeral from far off places were unfamiliar. She thought: Jim is the last of the family, except his brother Charlie, and Charlie is sick and almost blind. That must be Charlie's son, Harry, over there to the left. He has the same dark curly hair and he holds his head like Charlie did, sort of proud and elegant. That's his wife, sitting next to him, I expect, and those sitting next to her, now, they would be Sally Nat's daughter Patricia and her husband. She wished she dared turn around and have a good look at the faces of the well-dressed women sitting behind her. Well, she'd see them all when they went to the cemetery. She wondered where Jim would be buried. Good Lawd, not in the family lot.

Comfort, oh Lord, the loved ones of the deceased, especially the kind and loving brother who lies ill so far away.

Jim's nephew Harry felt a sudden, frightening rush of emotion, a wild desire to laugh aloud while his eyes filled with tears. Poor Dad; it's tough on him to lose his brother and not be able to be here, to be home in his sick-bed. Harry could see his father's face when they told him Jim was dead. Confined to his bed with a lingering illness and the feeble bones of old age, Charlie had said nothing, but the misery in Charlie's face told of the love he had for his black-sheep brother. Harry remembered Charley's stories, of how close the brothers were as boys. And stories about Sissie, four years older than Jim, and Aunt Sally Nat, who was three years younger than Charlie. The two boys, separated in age by only ten months, were united against the world and their sisters. "Closer than twins," Aunt Sissie used to say. In his mind, Harry could see the two brothers, as boys, playing together, his father, looking as Harry had always known him, neat, clean and handsome, and Uncle Jim, just as handsome, but seedy and dirty.

In the little room at the side of the undertaker's parlor, usually reserved for The Family, Kitty Horley sat beside her father and an aunt, listening to the undertaker's prayer:. "Comfort the brother." Her brightly painted lips drew into a tight line, her café au lait face darkened and her black eyes glittered. "Comfort the brother," she repeated in her mind. Not a word about asking the Lord to comfort the widow, the woman who was his common-law wife. Oh Lord, comfort this woman who was his common-law wife, this wench who lived with him, took care of him, toted his slops, nursed him as tenderly as a mother cared for her sick child; this nigger who dared to sleep with this great grandson of a pioneer settler, this son of a Confederate veteran, this member of an aristocratic family.

"Damn them," she cried to herself. "Damn them to hell."

The man she loved was gone. The white nieces and nephews, the white cousins and friends sat out in front listening to the undertaker. That last remaining brother—comfort the brother—had arranged for the undertaker to read the funeral service. Not even a preacher to bury Jim decently. And the undertaker prayed for that brother. Her heart was big within her and she choked back the sobs. Those white folks would not see her shed a tear. God, how she hated them, and hated the years during which she had walked the streets of Burnsville, head high and eyes on the distance, as white women looked scornfully at her and white men sniggered and tried to attract her attention.

For man walketh in a vain shadow and disquieteth himself; he heapeth up riches and cannot tell who shall gather them.

Genie Belle fidgeted in her chair in the second row. She tried to look at the flowers and guess who sent what. Were those white flowers roses or carnations? She could not be sure; Genie Belle's myopic eyes could scarcely bring into focus the face of her mother, seated beside her. Genie Belle's mind whirled. She half heard the undertaker as she tried to remember.

Something from long ago. About Uncle Dave. What did Uncle Dave Shane have to do with Jim's funeral? "Uncle Dave and his nigra wife. Uncle Dave and his nigra wife." Her mind kept going over the words. Who was it she kept trying to think of? Suddenly, she remembered. She had been sitting on the floor at home, not even ten years old, playing paper dolls and listening as her mother and Cousin Lizzie talked.

"It's scandalous," her mother had said, "but, somehow I can't help thinking it is right funny."

Cousin Lizzie had looked shocked, but Mama had gone on. "It was awful that Uncle Dave Shane had a nigra wife after his wife Peggy died. When his children moved out and quit speaking to him, he took his mother's portrait, that lovely oil painting, to hang in the house where he had put up That Woman. And they had children—two girls. But I can't help wishing I could have seen those Du Barron Girls when they went to that house to try to buy their grandmother's portrait—not that they told the Shane Nigras it was their grandmother—they just said they were interested in the painting. And the Shane Nigras told them they did not care to sell it, that, after all, it was a portrait of their grandmother too. Those Du Barron Girls are mighty rich and mighty prissy, and I can't help wishing I could have seen their faces. I do think it's right funny."

"But Cousin Geneva, it's horrible to think of Uncle Dave's mother's portrait hanging in that nigra house."

"Yes, Cousin Lizzie, I reckon it is horrible, but what Uncle Dave did was horrible, too, and I don't really know as I can blame the Shane Nigras."

Genie Belle's stomach turned over. So that was it. Uncle Dave, Cousin Jim's grandfather, also had a common-law wife, and like Cousin Jim, he had provided for her. Only, of course, Cousin Jim had nothing to provide until Aunt Sissie died and left him everything she had. Did Aunt Sissie know about the common-law wife? Genie Belle frowned and wondered.

Scion of an aristocratic family, the last of

*his family save the kind brother who lay ill in
a far-away city—*

Harry felt a wild desire to rise up from his chair and shout. Such
pretense. Such sham. Dammit, why must we pretend That Woman in
the Family Room is not there? I didn't even know about Her until Dad
got sick a few years back and told me to send that check every month.
He sure didn't seem to make much of Her at the time. That was before
Aunt Sissie died and left everything to Uncle Jim. I wonder what Uncle
Jim did about a will? Did he deed everything to her to try to protect the
family from the news of the will's probation? I probably could find out
if I went to the court house, but I won't. I can't. Everybody in town
would know, that was for certain. The ordinary's wife would tell her
friends and they'd tell their friends.

*The undertaker's tones were lugubrious. The
spotless white collar around his fat neck
wriggled a little as his Adam's apple moved up
and down. His black suit was brushed and
pressed; his eyes were closed reverently.*

Patricia, who sat beside her husband Joe, turned to exchange a
quick look with him. She knew Joe was thinking how strange it all was
and that he did not think things were funny, as she did, what with his
remembering Mother Sally Nat and her stern refusal to admit there was
a word of truth in the gossip. She knew Joe was wondering, again, what
would be the effect of the funeral. Would it start the town buzzing once
more with the talk that had sort of died down since everybody had been
gossiping about the shooting on Calhoun Street.

The undertaker's prayer continued.

But Cousin Lizzie did not hear it. She was sitting very straight in
the second row of seats, straining to look through the half-open door of
the Family Room, and she was trying to look as if she were not trying
to see who was in that room. I know she came to the funeral, Cousin
Lizzie thought. I wonder who came with her. I never heard of them
having any children.

Cousin Fannie was not listening to the service either. She was only
a fifth cousin, once removed, and she sat in the fifth row of chairs,
beside a friend who so obviously wanted to attend the funeral that there
was no way out of it, especially when she came to offer condolences
the evening before and said; "Fannie, you don't have a car. I'll come by
at ten o'clock and pick you up for the funeral." Cousin Fannie was torn

between anger at the outsiders who had come to the funeral out of curiosity, and gratitude to those old friends who had come out of an affectionate regard for the family and respect for the name that had stood high in the town for generations.

Old Colonel Tompkins made snorting noises behind his mustache and cleared his throat, tired of the undertaker. Dammed fool. Why did he have to go on? Didn't he KNOW about the widow, or was he trying to pretend there was nothing unusual about the funeral. Jim was a rascal, all right, and everybody knew he lived with that nigger wench and what was the use of pretending.

Kitty Horley's rage was gone. Only grief was with her, filling her soul, sickening her body, bringing a taste of nausea to her mouth, pushing a great lump of sorrow deep in her throat, misting with tears the dark eyes, and breaking her fine mullato face into a grimace she never meant the white folks to see. Through the half-heard words of the undertaker she let her mind go back to the days when Jim Horley first courted her. She was young and heedless and happy; she cared nothing for the sniggers of the Negroes who lived next door to the shack where she lived with her father and the younger children. She had slipped out, night after night, to spend hours with the handsome white man who was so tender, so passionate, so loving. But one day her father had called her in from the broken front steps where she sat dreaming of Jim.

"Kitty," he had said, "you've got to stop seein' that white man. The Ku Kluxers is ridin' and there'll be bad trouble for us." She was wild with fear, not of the stinking, miserable Ku Kluxers, but fear of losing the loving man she could not do without. But she could not bring terror to her family, could not be the cause of their death—or at best, their merciless whipping. That night, she told Jim. He swore. Those goddamned bastards, they slept where they pleased and just because they were whoring around with white bitches, nobody cared. But for him to love a colored girl; that was a different kettle of fish. They planned carefully. They left there together. Kitty closed her eyes and made a brief mental visit back to the house where they had lived in Detroit. They had stayed nearly ten years until the trouble had been mostly forgotten back home and Miss Sissie had died and left Jim everything she had. Did Miss Sissie know about what her brother had done, Kitty wondered.

For a thousand years in thy sight are as a yesterday; seeing that is past as a watch in the night.

Sara Watson fidgeted in her chair. What was all this funny business? Everybody not looking at anybody? All those quick looks toward the Family Room. Sara lived in a city two hundred miles from Burnsville and she had not heard the talk. She only knew that her invalid mother had burst into tears when she got the news of Great Uncle Jim's death and had moaned about what were people going to say about him, and she had declared Sara must go to the funeral. In spite of it all, he **was** their kinsman.

Sara had always known there was something strange about Uncle Jim. When Mamma had whispered to Papa and Sara had asked, "What?" Mama had told her to go out and play. But behind her she heard someone whisper over the undertaker's words: "Did you know that when Miss Sissie died and left everything to Jim, he bought that two-story house on Boddy's Lane and lived there with That Woman? He put everything in her name, too, just like his granddaddy Dave Shane."

Maybe I can find out at the cemetery who that woman is and what it's all about, Sara thought.

Cousin Lizzie leaned a little further forward in her chair and fanned herself with her turkey-tail fan. Even the new-fangled air conditioning did not keep her from breaking into a sweat. She HAD to get a look at That Woman. Cousin Lizzie had pointed Her out once, on the street. But that was years ago, before my husband died. Must have been at least 10 years now. They say she was good to Cousin Jim, but, Good Lord, wasn't it awful, him living out there with her like that.

The undertaker nodded to the pall bearers. The people stood up. The coffin was moved, not down the center aisle but out through the door at the right where The Family sat. Cousin Lizzie got a quick look at the handsome, overdressed mulatto, whose painted face and bright lips showed no trace of grief, not even an interest in the proceedings. The cars followed the hearse a few blocks down the paved streets and turned into the cemetery gate to drive along the shady dirt road, bordered with red cedars, oaks and magnolias. They passed the newer part of the cemetery where slept the dead of the newcomers who had lived scarce fifty years in the town, and moved on to the older section of the graveyard where family lots were planted with ancient box-wood and surrounded by iron fences of elaborate grillwork patterns. The cars stopped near the lot where Jim Horley's parents, grandparents and great-grandparents rested beneath marble slabs. Cousin Geneva, Cousin Lizze, Genie Belle—a handful of kinfolks and friends alighted from their cars and stood beside the grave, its red clay sides and the near-by mound of earth covered with the bright green artificial grass blanket with which the undertaker thought to alleviate the more frightening aspects of burial. While the white people stood waiting, a small car drew up and from it alighted three Negroes. Respectfully, they stood at one side. They might have been family servants at the funeral of any white person in town, and under other circumstances, nobody would have taken a second look at them.

Harry pressed his lips together hard. Doesn't it seem strange for Jim to be buried in the family burying ground, alongside an ancestor who fought with Lee, his aristocratic father, his mother who was a lady to her fingertips. I wonder where That Woman expects to be buried. Good God, not in the family plot beside Jim, of course. Although he could scarcely remember his grandmother, Harry visualized her; black silk dress, tight stays, cameo brooch, and an air of elegance that impressed even her grandchildren, her lips pressed tight in disapproval.

Man that is born of woman had but a short time to live and is full of misery.

Poor Jim. Was he full of misery? Cousin Geneva fluttered her fan and stole a look at the mulatto woman who stood beside a gray-haired, light-complexioned man, and an aged black woman. What misery had driven Jim to take a nigra wife?

Thou knowest, Oh Lord, the secrets of our hearts; shut not thy merciful ears.

Secrets. Cousin Lizzie could scarcely forbear a snort. There certainly was nothing secret about Cousin Jim's goings-on. Everybody talked about him, except his own family who only spoke of it in intimate moments and out of the hearing of the children.

Earth to earth, dust to dust, ashes to ashes. The undertaker's assistant dropped a few rose petals on the casket. The grace of our Lord, Jesus Christ, and the love and fellowship of the Holy Ghost be with us all evermore.

The group broke up silently, couples and threesomes moving toward the cars. There was not the usual speaking one to another, the talk in low mournful tones, the sympathetic handclasp, the questioning about Aunt Susie's or Uncle John's health, the comment on how much this or that one favored his papa. The cousins would meet at Cousin Geneva's for dinner, a little later, and there would be time enough for talk then. They wanted to get away from the grave and the presence of the common-law wife and the feeling of guilt that, somehow, sat heavily upon them.

Genie Belle moved slowly toward her car, walking with Cousin Lizzie and Colonel Tompkins. None of them spoke of the thing uppermost in the minds of all of them. Genie Belle nodded a goodbye as Cousin Lizzie turned to go to her automobile, accompanied by Colonel Tompkins.

"Y'all come on by the house after while," Genie Belle re-extended the invitation.

She reached her car and then discovered her mother was not close behind. She walked a few steps back around the curve which had hidden the grave from her view.

Genie Belle did not know for sure what she saw. She squinted, but her myopic eyes refused to clarify the distant figures. But she thought she saw the figure of the mulatto woman bowed in grief beside the grave, and Genie Belle was almost certain it was her mother who stood beside the bowed figure and put a comforting arm about the woman who was her common-law cousin.

———————————

Editor's Note: See Appendix II for more on interracial relationships.

APPENDIX I

The Myrick Family

The parents of these girls, James Dowdell Myrick and Thulia Katherine Whitehurst, married in April 2, 1879 and set up their first home at Myrick's Mill, a family plantation of 3700 acres in Twiggs County, Georgia, not far from Milledgeville. They spent much of their time, however, at his parents' home—the Rockwell Mansion—in a section of Milledgeville known as Midway. James took more and more responsibility for managing his father's properties as General Stith Parham Myrick aged. The family tried to hold onto the more profitable lands by letting the poorer ones go.

After his father's death in 1885, James and his family stayed at Midway while they built a new home on Myrick land in northwest Baldwin County, a site known as the Hurt Place, and renamed their new home "Dovedale." They went back in time to an earlier spelling of James's mother's family name "Dowdell." The spelling had evolved over time from Dovedale to Dowdale to Dowdall and finally to Dowdell.

When his mother died in 1889, James sold the Midway home, settled all outstanding debts, and began to devote his efforts to Dovedale Plantation, which family tradition says was purchased with Confederate money during the War Between the States..

The family grew to eight children, and the house expanded with the family.

James practiced soil conservation, diversified farming and crop rotation. He taught his tenant farmers to plant cover crops, to build terraces, and to plow with the contour of the land. These lessons became the foundation of the family's farming philosophy and in later years their daughter Susan became a leader in teaching these conservation principles to Southern farmers through her newspaper farm pages and articles in farming magazines.

Owning a cotton gin, he could hold his cotton when prices were low and sell when they rose again. He produced his own flour and cornmeal, grew, butchered and smoked his own meats, and raised a variety of fruits and vegetables. He installed a hydraulic ram to pipe water into the family home (long before electricity came to rural Georgia). He built and maintained a school for neighborhood children. Mrs. Myrick operated the Dovedale post office for the community, and ran a store for the plantation workers.

After James Dowdell died from complications of diabetes in November 1910, his family moved to Milledgeville and the Dovedale post office closed on February 15, 1911.

More details of the family can be obtained from: Allie M. Bowden's *The Story of the Myricks*, which should be available in genealogical libraries throughout the country.

APPENDIX II

Cousin Gus Myrick

Sue wrote "Who Shall Gather Them" about 1958-1960 and very likely based it on the life and death of a cousin, Gus Myrick. Gus met a black lady, Mary Harden, a widow with two children, when he moved to Wilkinson County. She became his common-law wife at a time when racial intermarriage was illegal in Georgia. They had no children. They remained together for more than 30 years, moving to various locations in Wilkinson and Baldwin counties and in Milledgeville. She died in February 1958. At that time, Mary's granddaughter Mildred Harden Huff took care of Gus, seeing that he had a live-in care giver; she also picked him up daily after leaving her full-time job, drove him to her family's home, and cooked him a solid meal. He died a few months later, in late spring. She and her family attended the funeral.

Like Jim Horley, Gus was considered the "black sheep" of the family and was talked about in whispers by the adults who sought to keep his life a secret from the children. As a child I would see Gus striding down the road to town or to work, a tall, bearded man. He is said to have shaved off his beard, but when no one recognized him, he let it grow out again. At one time, he did day labor on my family's farm.

His brother W. S. Myrick ran a dry-goods store in downtown Milledgeville and Gus worked in his store for a time. The brother sold the store and moved to Florida. He gave Gus a full suit, and the husband of Mary's granddaughter, Bennie Huff, said he probably wore it only to be buried in.

Bennie tells about his own great-grandfather, a white man, William Huff. William worked as overseer on the Humbler Plantation in Putnam County where he met a slave, Jane. He took her for his common-law wife and they had a total of 13 children, three born in Putnam County and ten in Baldwin County. H e purchased land near the Milledgeville-Macon road (the "lower" Macon road). There he married a white woman and had several children. His interracial children were all older than his white children; he gave the white children the same names he had given his interracial children.

Gus is buried in the family plot with the Stith Parham Myrick, General of the Georgia Militia and sponsor of the Myrick Volunteers in the War Between the States—scion of an aristocratic family of the Old South. Gus's grave is marked only with an un-inscribed slab.

Records of Bethel Church (See "Old Bethel) show that—

—an (illegible first name) August Myrick was baptized August 7, 1888.

The first name might be Thornton, but is unclear.

—Augustus Myrick joined the church on September 10, 1897 by certificate

—T. Augusts Myrick, joined by certificate, on September 15, 1897. He is also listed as joining on October 9, 1902 "because of an error in removal."

APPENDIX III

Dr. Hubert

Dr. Hubert purchased a farm that became home for the duration of his life. When he first got the home and land, he treated patients on the back porch until an office was completed in 1915. The building had two rooms, one for patients to wait, and one for treatment. The building was located next to the driveway and close to the corner of the main house.

After his death, Tippie moved to Milledgeville and sold the country place to Blanche Green Jordan Lumpkin, who passed it on to her daughter Valette Jordan. It became known then as Surrey Lane.

APPENDIX IV

Old Bethel

The Complete Church Register of Bethel Church, Baldwin Circuit, North Georgia conference, Methodist Episcopal Church, South, bears the original date of 1883.

It contains a copy of the deed from Samuel H. Hughes for a parcel of land "containing ten thousand square yards in the form of a square being one hundred yards in length on each side." He states that the gift is "for and in consideration of the love I bear for the Cause of Christ and from an earnest desire to promote that heritage on earth." The deed also grants the church a right of way to the spring and use of the spring.

A note in the records by J. D. Myrick, dated 1907, states: "The old Church building at Bethel was erected about 1813 as Mr. William Green says it stood 40 years. The present building was completed July 1853 & dedicated following November."

Above the "1853" is written "1945," the year the Sunday school rooms were added to the back of the building. The Bethel Church I attended as a youth and teenager burned and a new building was erected in 1968.

The records show that

—Aunt Lizzie Good (nee Lizzie Hawkins) joined by profession of faith in August 1888, married Goodwin D. Myrick on December 16, 1869, and died November 6, 1922.

—Susan S. Myrick and Allie G. Myrick joined August 1902 by profession of faith. (The "S." of Susan S. Myrick is very distinct, although handwritten.)

—Elizabeth (Tippie) S. Myrick, Susan D. Myrick and Allie Goodwin Myrick were baptized April 18, 1896

APPENDIX IV

The Rockwell Mansion

Samuel Rockwell, a New York attorney, moved to Milledgeville when it was the capitol and built his home on Allen Memorial Drive in the Midway community of Milledgeville. The exact date is unknown. Descendents of the family put the date at 1829, while the Winterthur Museum puts the date at 1837. The Nomination papers for the Mansion to the National Register of Historic Places dates the house to 1838 on the basis of the increase in value of Rockwell's properties on the tax digest for Baldwin County between 1838 and 1839.

The Greek revival mansion was designed by Joseph Lane, Senior, who came to Georgia with Rockwell. Lane also designed the Central Building at Oglethorpe University in Milledgeville.

The house was sold several times; about 1850 it was purchased by Herschel V. Johnson, governor of Georgia. Stith Parham Myrick became the next resident. His son James Dowdell Myrick sold the house after the death of both of his parents.

In 1969, after a fire damaged part of the house, Winterthur Museum purchased the dining room. They removed the black marble mantle and all the woodwork: wainscoting, door facings and the sliding panel doors between the dining and living rooms. The owner would not sell the flooring.

The Museum also purchased impressions of the decorative plaster around the ceiling and the central medallion.

Winterthur Museum is located near Wilmington, Delaware. Further information about the museum can be obtained from the museum's web site: www.winterthur.org.

More information about the Rockwell Mansion can be obtained from a term paper, "Beaumont" by Douglas Wayne Etheridge, August 1974, which is in the Hardy Architectural Class Papers housed in the archives at the Special Collections Library of Georgia College and State University in Milledgeville, Georgia.

APPENDIX V

Myrick's Mill

Myrick's Mill was built some time before 1825 and consisted of about 3,700 acres. It passed from Stith Parham Myrick to James Dowdell Myrick, and eventually to the Napier family of Putman County. The Napier family owned a grist mill a mile or two from the Dovedale Plantation house, on Little Cedar Creek, so the families were friends and neighbors.

Myrick's Mill has been described as "a three storied structure that once housed five large stone mills for making corn meal and wheat flour."

In 1825, Marquis de Lafayette visited the mill, and after returning to France, he sent the miller a piece of silk so the mill could bolt its flour.

Sherman's troops came within ten miles of the mill.

The mill was powered by water from a 75-acre lake. The water was channeled through two turbines that rotated shafts attached to pulleys and belts that turned the mill stones.

The Georgia Historical Commission placed a marker on the site in 1954.

Further information can be obtained from the web site www.myricksmill.com, the web site of Billy Humphries whose grandfather purchased the property in the 1920s.

**Tippie with daughter Ann
About 1906**

**Tippie & Dr. Hubert
about 1940**

Thulia Whitehurst Myrick, 1933

Thulia Katherine Whitehurst at time of marriage

Sue (right) and friend at Liberty Street House

**Sue (left, rear) member of honorary society at the
Normal School of Physical Education, Battle Creek, 1914**

Sue, at her apartment house in Macon, 1944

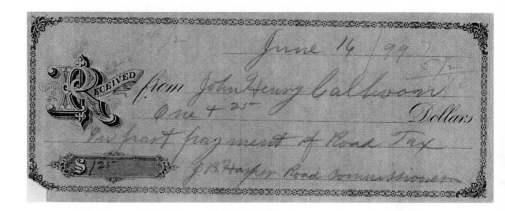

County tax receipt for Sherman

John C. Calhoun (Sherman)

LANDLORD'S LIEN.   FORM NO. 26.   Louisville, (Ga.,) News & Farmer Job Print.

STATE OF GEORGIA, *Baldwin* COUNTY.

THIS AGREEMENT, Made and executed this *6* day of *July 1900* 189_

between *James D Myrick* Landlord, and

Jessie Freeman his tenant doth witness, that in consideration of the said

James D Myrick Landlord, furnishing the said

Jessie Freeman supplies, money, farming utensils, or

other articles necessary to make crops; clothing, medicines and articles of necessity to supply a family, or any of said

articles, during the year 1900, not exceeding *Ninety five* Dollars

he hereby obligates himself to pay the same on the *15th* day of *October* 1900

And in order to secure the said *James D Myrick* Landlord, or assigns, in making

the said advances, I, the said *Jessie Freeman* hereby create and give to the

said *James D Myrick* Landlord, and his assigns, a full and complete lien on my entire

crop of corn, cotton and all other produce growning or to be grown by me during the year 1900, on the land in said County whereupon I farm during said year. I further affirm that this is the only lien given by me on said Crop.

I AGREE, that should this lien have to be enforced by law, to pay ten per cent. Attorney's fees and Court costs. As against this debt I waive all my rights to Homestead or exemptions allowed under the Laws of Georgia.

IN TESTIMONY of all all of which, I have hereto set my hand and seal, the day and year first above written.

Executed in presence of:

John Henry Jackson   *Jessie X Freeman* [SEAL.]
                                                                    mark

_____   _____ [SEAL.]

Tenant lease at Dovedale Plantation

Rockwell Mansion in 2000

Lil (right) at GN&IC campus

Dovedale post office and store, about 1950

Myrick's Mill, about 1961, painting by Katie Myrick Lowerre

Elizabeth Dowdell Myrick (Mrs. S. P.)

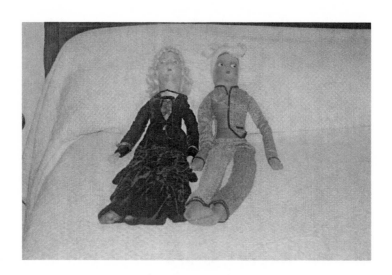

Lil's dolls

Nan Whitehurst and Lil

Lil (center front) with friends and Tinker Bell

Lil in front of Liberty Street House

Lil and Tinker Bell

James Dowdell Myrick

Historic marker at site of Myrick's Mill

**Stith Parham Myrick in uniform as General
in Georgia Militia at time of the War Between the States**

No. 2011.

Post Office Department,

OFFICE OF THE SECOND ASSISTANT POSTMASTER GENERAL,

CONTRACT DIVISION,

Washington, D. C., _____, 190___

Sir:

The following is the schedule of departures and arrivals of the mail on Route

No. *21511*, of which ——S. N. RANGELEY—————————— is the

Contractor; ordered to take effect *at once*_____, 190___

Leave *Dovedale* _____ at *7.30 am*

Arrive at *Meriwether* _____ by *10.50*

Leave _____''_____ { *after arrival of mail from Atlanta but not later than 3 pm*

Arrive at *Dovedale* _____ *in 1½ hours.*

Leave _____

Arrive at _____

Leave _____

Arrive at _____

When service is less than six times a week, and a failure occurs on schedule day, the mail should be carried on the first day possible thereafter.

Report to the DIVISION OF INSPECTION of this Office EVERY FAILURE of the mail to depart as above required, and EVERY FAILURE to arrive at the time above set.

☞ Registers of arrival and departure of the mail should be addressed, SECOND ASSISTANT POSTMASTER GENERAL, DIVISION OF INSPECTION, WASHINGTON, D. C.

Very respectfully,

W. D. Shallenberger .
_____
Second Assistant Postmaster General.

Postmaster at *Dovedale*,

Baldwin Co.,

Ga.

5—415

1937   OlIVE   MARTHA   Al   VANCOUVER

DRESSED ACCORDING TO OCCASION

Uniforms at GN&IC

Allie, Columbus, GA 1933   **Allie**

Also by Susan Lindsley from ThomasMax Publishing:

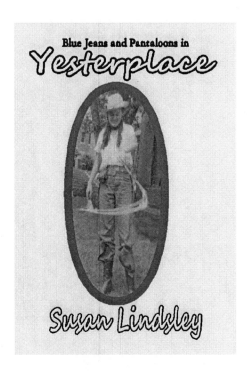

Blue Jeans and Pantaloons in Yesterplace

Yesterplace inhabitants included Flannery O'Connor, Susan Myrick of Gone With The Wind, cattle rustlers, shady politicians, world-renown scientists, murders and a conjure woman. With neither television nor telephone, Susan and her sisters made up their games and songs, rode horses to the picture show, and played at Roy Rogers and Jesse James. Yesterplace won the Josephine Mellichamp Award for nonfiction from the Southeastern Writers Association.

Only $16.00. Available almost everywhere books are sold. If your favorite store doesn't have the book in stock, ask the store to order it for you. Also available through most internet sellers, including Amazon.com and Barnes & Noble's website, or purchase the book directly from the publisher (free shipping in the U.S.) via Paypal at thomasmax.com.

SUSAN MYRICK

OF

GONE WITH THE WIND

An Autobiographical Biography

SUSAN LINDSLEY

***After Midnight in Savannah* by B. Forrest Spink**

Reverend Alva Martin was murdered in her home in December, 1991. Her son, Jim, was subsequently convicted of her murder in what appeared to be an open-and-shut case of a crack-addicted son killing his mother so he could sell her things to buy more drugs. The son, however, insists more than a decade later that he was not the killer, that the murder was committed by his drug supplier, an African-American female impersonator. Lots of insight into a dysfunctional mother/son relationship (she was a Nazarene minister, he was a homosexual with a kinky side). Includes transcripts of the trial, interviews with the convicted son, an aunt and the officer who met with the accused on the night of the murder. $12.95.

CPSIA information can be obtained at www.ICGtesting.com
Printed in the USA
LVOW13s1957250414

383292LV00001B/120/P

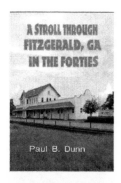

A Stroll Through Fitzgerald, GA, In The Forties by Paul B. Dunn, $14.95. Take an imaginary stroll through the streets of Fitzgerald, Georgia, in the post-World War II era. The walk may be imaginary, but the streets, the businesses, the people -- and the atmosphere of a simpler era -- are all very real.

Lightning Slinger of Andersonville by Paul B. Dunn, $14.95. The story of Teddie O'Dunn, a telegrapher-depot agent who began his career on the railroad in Andersonville, then moved to Fitzgerald, a colony city comprised of Yankees and southerners. Warned to stay away from Yankee girls in Fitzgerald, Teddie was "lightning struck" by the granddaughter of a cavalryman in General Sherman's Army. $14.95. A companion book about Teddie's wife, *Tremble Chin*, is also available by Dunn for $14.95.

Walk With Me by J.D. Lankford, $11.95. Take a walk with Broxton, Georgia's J.D. Lankford through the hard times of the Great Depression, through his work in the CCC and through his Army career, including his time as a Prisoner of War in Nazi Germany. After returning home and getting married, he re-enlisted and was dispatched to Korea, where he earned 5 bronze stars to go with the 4 he had earned in World War II. Some anecdotes are amusing, but many more are horrific and he warns the reader who walks with him: "Don't get involved. You won't like it."

We Enjoyed Alaska But Russell Just About Killed Us by Julian Anderson Williams, $13.95. How did Alaska's Supreme Court Chief Justice wind up in an unlikely grave near a rural Georgia road? Broxton's Julian Williams wanted to know and signed on for a 31-day tour that included Alaska. He and his wife learned a lot about Justice Boney and had a grand experience on the tour, an experience tempered by the vinegar and spice of a reluctant fellow traveler, Russell Collins, who contended that all history and progress of Alaska were subject to his interpretation.